The Birds by Aristophanes

Translated from the Greek.

The reality is that little is known of Aristophanes actual life but eleven of his forty plays survive intact and upon those rest his deserved reputation as the Father of Comedy or, The Prince of Ancient Comedy.

Accounts agree that he was born sometime between 456BC and 446 BC. Many cities claim the honor of his birthplace and the most probable story makes him the son of Philippus of Ægina, and therefore only an adopted citizen of Athens, a distinction which, at times could be cruel, though he was raised and educated in Athens.

His plays are said to recreate the life of ancient Athens more realistically than any other author could. Intellectually his powers of ridicule were feared by his influential contemporaries; Plato himself singled out Aristophanes' play The Clouds as a slander that contributed to the trial and condemning to death of Socrates and although other satirical playwrights had also caricatured the philosopher his carried the most weight.

His now lost play, The Babylonians, was denounced by the demagogue Cleon as a slander against the Athenian polis. Aristophanes seems to have taken this criticism to heart and thereafter caricatured Cleon mercilessly in his subsequent plays, especially The Knights.

His life and playwriting years were undoubtedly long though again accounts as to the year of his death vary quite widely. What can be certain is that his legacy of surviving plays is in effect both a treasured legacy but also in itself the only surviving texts of Ancient Greek comedy.

Index of Contents

Introduction
The Persons
Scene
THE BIRDS
Aristophanes – A Short Biography
Aristophanes – A Concise Bibliography

INTRODUCTION

'The Birds' differs markedly from all the other Comedies of Aristophanes which have come down to us in subject and general conception. It is just an extravaganza pure and simple—a graceful, whimsical theme chosen expressly for the sake of the opportunities it afforded of bright, amusing dialogue, pleasing lyrical interludes, and charming displays of brilliant stage effects and pretty dresses. Unlike other plays of the same Author, there is here apparently no serious political MOTIF underlying the surface burlesque and buffoonery.

Some critics, it is true, profess to find in it a reference to the unfortunate Sicilian Expedition, then in progress, and a prophecy of its failure and the political downfall of Alcibiades. But as a matter of fact, the whole thing seems rather an attempt on the dramatist's part to relieve the overwrought minds of his fellow-citizens, anxious and discouraged at the unsatisfactory reports from before Syracuse, by a work conceived in a lighter vein than usual and mainly unconnected with contemporary realities. The play was produced in the year 414 B.C., just when success or failure in Sicily hung in the balance, though already the outlook was gloomy, and many circumstances pointed to impending disaster. Moreover, the public conscience was still shocked and perturbed over the mysterious affair of the mutilation of the Hermae, which had occurred immediately before the sailing of the fleet, and strongly suspicious of Alcibiades' participation in the outrage. In spite of the inherent charm of the subject, the splendid outbursts of lyrical poetry in some of the choruses and the beauty of the scenery and costumes, 'The Birds' failed to win the first prize. This was acclaimed to a play of Aristophanes' rival, Amipsias, the title of which, 'The Comastoe,' or 'Revellers,' "seems to imply that the chief interest was derived from direct allusions to the outrage above mentioned and to the individuals suspected to have been engaged in it."

For this reason, which militated against its immediate success, viz. the absence of direct allusion to contemporary politics—there are, of course, incidental references here and there to topics and personages of the day—the play appeals perhaps more than any other of our Author's productions to the modern reader. Sparkling wit, whimsical fancy, poetic charm, are of all ages, and can be appreciated as readily by ourselves as by an Athenian audience of two thousand years ago, though, of course, much is inevitably lost "without the important adjuncts of music, scenery, dresses and what we may call 'spectacle' generally, which we know in this instance to have been on the most magnificent scale."

The plot is this. Euelpides and Pisthetaerus, two old Athenians, disgusted with the litigiousness, wrangling and sycophancy of their countrymen, resolve upon quitting Attica. Having heard of the fame of Epops (the hoopoe), sometime called Tereus, and now King of the Birds, they determine, under the direction of a raven and a jackdaw, to seek from him and his subject birds a city free from all care and strife. Arrived at the Palace of Epops, they knock, and Trochilus (the wren), in a state of great flutter, as he mistakes them for fowlers, opens the door and informs them that his Majesty is asleep. When he awakes, the strangers appear before him, and after listening to a long and eloquent harangue on the superior attractions of a residence among the birds, they propose a notable scheme of their own to further enhance its advantages and definitely secure the sovereignty of the universe now exercised by the gods of Olympus.

The birds are summoned to meet in general council. They come flying up from all quarters of the heavens, and after a brief mis-understanding, during which they come near tearing the two human envoys to pieces, they listen to the exposition of the latters' plan. This is nothing less than the building of a new city, to be called Nephelococcygia, or 'Cloud-cuckoo-town,' between earth and heaven, to be garrisoned and guarded by the birds in such a way as to intercept all communication of the gods with their worshippers on earth. All steam of sacrifice will be prevented from rising to Olympus, and the Immortals will very soon be starved into an acceptance of any terms proposed. The new Utopia is duly constructed, and the daring plan to secure the sovereignty is in a fair way to succeed. Meantime various quacks and charlatans, each with a special scheme for improving things, arrive from earth, and are one after the other exposed and dismissed. Presently arrives Prometheus, who informs Epops of the desperate straits to which the gods are by this time reduced, and advises him to push his claims and demand the hand of Basileia (Dominion), the handmaid of Zeus. Next an embassy from the Olympians appears on the scene, consisting of Heracles, Posidon and a god from the savage regions of the Triballians. After some disputation, it is agreed that all reasonable demands of the birds are to be granted, while Pisthetaerus is to have Basileia as his bride. The comedy winds up with the epithalamium in honour of the nuptials.

EUELPIDES
PISTHETAERUS
EPOPS (the Hoopoe)
TROCHILUS, Servant to Epops
PHOENICOPTERUS
HERALDS
A PRIEST
A POET
A PROPHET
METON, a Geometrician
A COMMISSIONER
A DEALER IN DECREES
IRIS
A PARRICIDE
CINESIAS, a Dithyrambic Bard
AN INFORMER
PROMETHEUS
POSIDON
TRIBALLUS
HERACLES
SLAVES OF PISTHETAERUS
MESSENGERS
CHORUS
OF BIRDS

SCENE

A wild, desolate tract of open country; broken rocks and brushwood occupy the centre of the stage.

EUELPIDES [To his **JAY**] (1)
Do you think I should walk straight for yon tree?

(1) EUELPIDES is holding a jay and PISTHETAERUS a crow; they are the guides who are to lead them to the kingdom of the birds.

PISTHETAERUS [To his **CROW**]
Cursed beast, what are you croaking to me?... to retrace my steps?

EUELPIDES
Why, you wretch, we are wandering at random, we are exerting ourselves only to return to the same spot; 'tis labour lost.

PISTHETAERUS

To think that I should trust to this crow, which has made me cover more than a thousand furlongs!

EUELPIDES
And that I to this jay, which has torn every nail from my fingers!

PISTHETAERUS
If only I knew where we were....

EUELPIDES
Could you find your country again from here?

PISTHETAERUS
No, I feel quite sure I could not, any more than could Execestides(1) find his.

(1) A stranger who wanted to pass as an Athenian, although coming originally for a far-away barbarian country.

EUELPIDES
Oh dear! oh dear!

PISTHETAERUS
Aye, aye, my friend, 'tis indeed the road of "oh dears" we are following.

EUELPIDES
That Philocrates, the bird-seller, played us a scurvy trick, when he pretended these two guides could help us to find Tereus,(1) the Epops, who is a bird, without being born of one. He has indeed sold us this jay, a true son of Tharelides,(2) for an obolus, and this crow for three, but what can they do? Why, nothing whatever but bite and scratch!—What's the matter with you then, that you keep opening your beak? Do you want us to fling ourselves headlong down these rocks? There is no road that way.

(1) A king of Thrace, a son of Ares, who married Procne, the daughter of Pandion, King of Athens, whom he had assisted against the Megarians. He violated his sister-in-law, Philomela, and then cut out her tongue; she nevertheless managed to convey to her sister how she had been treated. They both agreed to kill Itys, whom Procne had borne to Tereus, and dished up the limbs of his own son to the father; at the end of the meal Philomela appeared and threw the child's head upon the table. Tereus rushed with drawn sword upon the princesses, but all the actors in this terrible scene were metamorphosed. Tereus became an Epops (hoopoe), Procne a swallow, Philomela a nightingale, and Itys a goldfinch. According to Anacreon and Apollodorus it was Procne who became the nightingale and Philomela the swallow, and this is the version of the tradition followed by Aristophanes.

(2) An Athenian who had some resemblance to a jay.

PISTHETAERUS
Not even the vestige of a track in any direction.

EUELPIDES
And what does the crow say about the road to follow?

PISTHETAERUS
By Zeus, it no longer croaks the same thing it did.

EUELPIDES

And which way does it tell us to go now?

PISTHETAERUS

It says that, by dint of gnawing, it will devour my fingers.

EUELPIDES

What misfortune is ours! we strain every nerve to get to the birds,(1) do everything we can to that end, and we cannot find our way! Yes, spectators, our madness is quite different from that of Sacas. He is not a citizen, and would fain be one at any cost; we, on the contrary, born of an honourable tribe and family and living in the midst of our fellow-citizens, we have fled from our country as hard as ever we could go. 'Tis not that we hate it; we recognize it to be great and rich, likewise that everyone has the right to ruin himself; but the crickets only chirrup among the fig-trees for a month or two, whereas the Athenians spend their whole lives in chanting forth judgments from their law-courts.(2) That is why we started off with a basket, a stew-pot and some myrtle boughs(3) and have come to seek a quiet country in which to settle. We are going to Tereus, the Epops, to learn from him, whether, in his aerial flights, he has noticed some town of this kind.

(1) Literally, 'to go to the crows,' a proverbial expression equivalent to our 'going to the devil.'

(2) They leave Athens because of their hatred of lawsuits and informers; this is the especial failing of the Athenians satirized in 'The Wasps.'

(3) Myrtle boughs were used in sacrifices, and the founding of every colony was started by a sacrifice.

PISTHETAERUS

Here! look!

EUELPIDES

What's the matter?

PISTHETAERUS

Why, the crow has been pointing me to something up there for some time now.

EUELPIDES

And the jay is also opening its beak and craning its neck to show me I know not what. Clearly, there are some birds about here. We shall soon know, if we kick up a noise to start them.

PISTHETAERUS

Do you know what to do? Knock your leg against this rock.

EUELPIDES

And you your head to double the noise.

PISTHETAERUS

Well then use a stone instead; take one and hammer with it.

EUELPIDES

Good idea! Ho there, within! Slave! slave!

PISTHETAERUS

What's that, friend! You say, "slave," to summon Epops! It would be much better to shout, "Epops, Epops!"

EUELPIDES

Well then, Epops! Must I knock again? Epops!

TROCHILUS

Who's there? Who calls my master?

PISTHETAERUS

Apollo the Deliverer! What an enormous beak!(1)

(1) The actors wore masks made to resemble the birds they were supposed to represent.

TROCHILUS

Good god! they are bird-catchers.

EUELPIDES

The mere sight of him petrifies me with terror. What a horrible monster.

TROCHILUS

Woe to you!

EUELPIDES

But we are not men.

TROCHILUS

What are you, then?

EUELPIDES

I am the Fearling, an African bird.

TROCHILUS

You talk nonsense.

EUELPIDES

Well, then, just ask it of my feet.(1)

(1) Fear had had disastrous effects upon Euelpides' internal economy, and this his feet evidenced.

TROCHILUS

And this other one, what bird is it?

PISTHETAERUS

I? I am a Cackling, from the land of the pheasants.

EUELPIDES

But you yourself, in the name of the gods! what animal are you?

TROCHILUS

Why, I am a slave-bird.

EUELPIDES
Why, have you been conquered by a cock?

TROCHILUS
No, but when my master was turned into a peewit, he begged me to become a bird too, to follow and to serve him.

EUELPIDES
Does a bird need a servant, then?

TROCHILUS
'Tis no doubt because he was a man. At times he wants to eat a dish of loach from Phalerum; I seize my dish and fly to fetch him some. Again he wants some pea-soup; I seize a ladle and a pot and run to get it.

EUELPIDES
This is, then, truly a running-bird.(1) Come, Trochilus, do us the kindness to call your master.

(1) The Greek word for a wren is derived from the same root as 'to run.'

TROCHILUS
Why, he has just fallen asleep after a feed of myrtle-berries and a few grubs.

EUELPIDES
Never mind; wake him up.

TROCHILUS
I an certain he will be angry. However, I will wake him to please you.

PISTHETAERUS
You cursed brute! why, I am almost dead with terror!

EUELPIDES
Oh! my god! 'twas sheer fear that made me lose my jay.

PISTHETAERUS
Ah! you great coward! were you so frightened that you let go your jay?

EUELPIDES
And did you not lose your crow, when you fell sprawling on the ground? Pray tell me that.

PISTHETAERUS
No, no.

EUELPIDES
Where is it, then?

PISTHETAERUS
It has flown away.

EUELPIDES

Then you did not let it go? Oh! you brave fellow!

EPOPS

Open the forest, that I may go out!

EUELPIDES

By Heracles! what a creature! what plumage! What means this triple crest?

EPOPS

Who wants me?

EUELPIDES

The twelve great gods have used you ill, meseems.

EPOPS

Are you chaffing me about my feathers? I have been a man, strangers.

EUELPIDES

'Tis not you we are jeering at.

EPOPS

At what, then?

EUELPIDES

Why, 'tis your beak that looks so odd to us.

EPOPS

This is how Sophocles outrages me in his tragedies. Know, I once was Tereus.

EUELPIDES

You were Tereus, and what are you now? a bird or a peacock?

EPOPS

I am a bird.

EUELPIDES

Then where are your feathers? For I don't see them.

EPOPS

They have fallen off.

EUELPIDES

Through illness?

EPOPS

No. All birds moult their feathers, you know, every winter, and others grow in their place. But tell me, who are you?

EUELPIDES

We? We are mortals.

EPOPS
From what country?

EUELPIDES
From the land of the beautiful galleys.(1)

(1) Athens.

EPOPS
Are you dicasts?(1)

(1) The Athenians were addicted to lawsuits. (See 'The Wasps.')

EUELPIDES
No, if anything, we are anti-dicasts.

EPOPS
Is that kind of seed sown among you?

EUELPIDES
You have to look hard to find even a little in our fields.

EPOPS
What brings you here?

EUELPIDES
We wish to pay you a visit.

EPOPS
What for?

EUELPIDES
Because you formerly were a man, like we are, formerly you had debts, as we have, formerly you did not want to pay them, like ourselves; furthermore, being turned into a bird, you have when flying seen all lands and seas. Thus you have all human knowledge as well as that of birds. And hence we have come to you to beg you to direct us to some cosy town, in which one can repose as if on thick coverlets.

EPOPS
And are you looking for a greater city than Athens?

EUELPIDES
No, not a greater, but one more pleasant to dwell in.

EPOPS
Then you are looking for an aristocratic country.

EUELPIDES
I? Not at all! I hold the son of Scellias in horror.(1)

(1) His name was Aristocrates; he was a general and commanded a fleet sent in aid of Corcyra.

EPOPS
But, after all, what sort of city would please you best?

EUELPIDES
A place where the following would be the most important business transacted.—Some friend would come knocking at the door quite early in the morning saying, "By Olympian Zeus, be at my house early, as soon as you have bathed, and bring your children too. I am giving a nuptial feast, so don't fail, or else don't cross my threshold when I am in distress."

EPOPS
Ah! that's what may be called being fond of hardships! And what say you?

PISTHETAERUS
My tastes are similar.

EPOPS
And they are?

PISTHETAERUS
I want a town where the father of a handsome lad will stop in the street and say to me reproachfully as if I had failed him, "Ah! Is this well done, Stilbonides! You met my son coming from the bath after the gymnasium and you neither spoke to him, nor embraced him, nor took him with you, nor ever once twitched his parts. Would anyone call you an old friend of mine?"

EPOPS
Ah! wag, I see you are fond of suffering. But there is a city of delights, such as you want. 'Tis on the Red Sea.

EUELPIDES
Oh, no. Not a sea-port, where some fine morning the Salaminian galley can appear, bringing a writ-server along. Have you no Greek town you can propose to us?

EPOPS
Why not choose Lepreum in Elis for your settlement?

EUELPIDES
By Zeus! I could not look at Lepreum without disgust, because of Melanthius.(1)

(1) A tragic poet, who was a leper; there is a play, of course, on the word Lepreum.

EPOPS
Then, again, there is the Opuntian, where you could live.

EUELPIDES
I would not be Opuntian(1) for a talent. But come, what is it like to live with the birds? You should know pretty well.

(1) An allusion to Opuntius, who was one-eyed.

EPOPS

Why, 'tis not a disagreeable life. In the first place, one has no purse.

EUELPIDES

That does away with much roguery.

EPOPS

For food the gardens yield us white sesame, myrtle-berries, poppies and mint.

EUELPIDES

Why, 'tis the life of the newly-wed indeed.(1)

(1) The newly-married ate a sesame-cake, decorated with garlands of myrtle, poppies and mint.

PISTHETAERUS

Ha! I am beginning to see a great plan, which will transfer the supreme power to the birds, if you will but take my advice.

EPOPS

Take your advice? In what way?

PISTHETAERUS

In what way? Well, firstly, do not fly in all directions with open beak; it is not dignified. Among us, when we see a thoughtless man, we ask, "What sort of bird is this?" and Teleas answers, "'Tis a man who has no brain, a bird that has lost his head, a creature you cannot catch, for it never remains in any one place."

EPOPS

By Zeus himself! your jest hits the mark. What then is to be done?

PISTHETAERUS

Found a city.

EPOPS

We birds? But what sort of city should we build?

PISTHETAERUS

Oh, really, really! 'tis spoken like a fool! Look down.

EPOPS

I am looking.

PISTHETAERUS

Now look upwards.

EPOPS

I am looking.

PISTHETAERUS

Turn your head round.

EPOPS

Ah! 'twill be pleasant for me, if I end in twisting my neck!

PISTHETAERUS

What have you seen?

EPOPS

The clouds and the sky.

PISTHETAERUS

Very well! is not this the pole of the birds then?

EPOPS

How their pole?

PISTHETAERUS

Or, if you like it, the land. And since it turns and passes through the whole universe, it is called, 'pole.' If you build and fortify it, you will turn your pole into a fortified city. In this way you will reign over mankind as you do over the grasshoppers and cause the gods to die of rabid hunger.

EPOPS

How so?

PISTHETAERUS

The air is 'twixt earth and heaven. When we want to go to Delphi, we ask the Boeotians(1) for leave of passage; in the same way, when men sacrifice to the gods, unless the latter pay you tribute, you exercise the right of every nation towards strangers and don't allow the smoke of the sacrifices to pass through your city and territory.

(1) Boeotia separated Attica from Phocis.

EPOPS

By earth! by snares! by network! I never heard of anything more cleverly conceived; and, if the other birds approve, I am going to build the city along with you.

PISTHETAERUS

Who will explain the matter to them?

EPOPS

You must yourself. Before I came they were quite ignorant, but since I have lived with them I have taught them to speak.

PISTHETAERUS

But how can they be gathered together?

EPOPS

Easily. I will hasten down to the coppice to waken my dear Procne! as soon as they hear our voices, they will come to us hot wing.

PISTHETAERUS

My dear bird, lose no time, I beg. Fly at once into the coppice and awaken Procne.

EPOPS
Chase off drowsy sleep, dear companion. Let the sacred hymn gush from thy divine throat in melodious strains; roll forth in soft cadence your refreshing melodies to bewail the fate of Itys, which has been the cause of so many tears to us both. Your pure notes rise through the thick leaves of the yew-tree right up to the throne of Zeus, where Phoebus listens to you, Phoebus with his golden hair. And his ivory lyre responds to your plaintive accents; he gathers the choir of the gods and from their immortal lips rushes a sacred chant of blessed voices.

[The flute is played in the background.

PISTHETAERUS
Oh! by Zeus! what a throat that little bird possesses. He has filled the whole coppice with honey-sweet melody!

EUELPIDES
Hush!

PISTHETAERUS
What's the matter?

EUELPIDES
Will you keep silence?

PISTHETAERUS
What for?

EUELPIDES
Epops is going to sing again.

EPOPS [In the coppice]
Epopoi poi popoi, epopoi, popoi, here, here, quick, quick, quick, my comrades in the air; all you who pillage the fertile lands of the husbandmen, the numberless tribes who gather and devour the barley seeds, the swift flying race who sing so sweetly. And you whose gentle twitter resounds through the fields with the little cry of tio, tio, tio, tio, tio, tio, tio, tio; and you who hop about the branches of the ivy in the gardens; the mountain birds, who feed on the wild olive berries or the arbutus, hurry to come at my call, trioto, trioto, totobrix; you also, who snap up the sharp-stinging gnats in the marshy vales, and you who dwell in the fine plain of Marathon, all damp with dew, and you, the francolin with speckled wings; you too, the halcyons, who flit over the swelling waves of the sea, come hither to hear the tidings; let all the tribes of long-necked birds assemble here; know that a clever old man has come to us, bringing an entirely new idea and proposing great reforms. Let all come to the debate here, here, here, here. Torotorotorotorotix, kikkobau, kikkobau, torotorotorotorolililix.

PISTHETAERUS
Can you see any bird?

EUELPIDES
By Phoebus, no! and yet I am straining my eyesight to scan the sky.

PISTHETAERUS

'Twas really not worth Epops' while to go and bury himself in the thicket like a plover when a-hatching.

PHOENICOPTERUS
Torotina, torotina.

PISTHETAERUS
Hold, friend, here is another bird.

EUELPIDES
I' faith, yes, 'tis a bird, but of what kind? Isn't it a peacock?

PISTHETAERUS
Epops will tell us. What is this bird?

EPOPS
'Tis not one of those you are used to seeing; 'tis a bird from the marshes.

PISTHETAERUS
Oh! oh! but he is very handsome with his wings as crimson as flame.

EPOPS
Undoubtedly; indeed he is called flamingo.(1)

(1) An African bird, that comes to the southern countries of Europe, to Greece, Italy, and Spain; it is even seen in Provence.

EUELPIDES
Hi! I say! You!

PISTHETAERUS
What are you shouting for?

EUELPIDES
Why, here's another bird.

PISTHETAERUS
Aye, indeed; 'tis a foreign bird too. What is this bird from beyond the mountains with a look as solemn as it is stupid?

EPOPS
He is called the Mede.(1)

(1) Aristophanes amusingly mixes up real birds with people and individuals, whom he represents in the form of birds; he is personifying the Medians here.

PISTHETAERUS
The Mede! But, by Heracles, how, if a Mede, has he flown here without a camel?

EUELPIDES
Here's another bird with a crest.

PISTHETAERUS

Ah! that's curious. I say, Epops, you are not the only one of your kind then?

EPOPS

This bird is the son of Philocles, who is the son of Epops; so that, you see, I am his grandfather; just as one might say, Hipponicus, the son of Callias, who is the son of Hipponicus.

PISTHETAERUS

Then this bird is Callias! Why, what a lot of his feathers he has lost!

EPOPS

That's because he is honest; so the informers set upon him and the women too pluck out his feathers.

PISTHETAERUS

By Posidon, do you see that many-coloured bird? What is his name?

EPOPS

This one? 'Tis the glutton.

PISTHETAERUS

Is there another glutton besides Cleonymus? But why, if he is Cleonymus, has he not thrown away his crest? But what is the meaning of all these crests? Have these birds come to contend for the double stadium prize?

EPOPS

They are like the Carians, who cling to the crests of their mountains for greater safety.

PISTHETAERUS

Oh, Posidon! do you see what swarms of birds are gathering
here?

EUELPIDES

By Phoebus! what a cloud! The entrance to the stage is no longer visible, so closely do they fly together.

PISTHETAERUS

Here is the partridge.

EUELPIDES

Faith! there is the francolin.

PISTHETAERUS

There is the poachard.

EUELPIDES

Here is the kingfisher. And over yonder?

EPOPS

'Tis the barber.

EUELPIDES

What? a bird a barber?

PISTHETAERUS

Why, Sporgilus is one. Here comes the owl.

EUELPIDES

And who is it brings an owl to Athens?(1)

(1) The owl was dedicated to Athene, and being respected at Athens, it had greatly multiplied. Hence the proverb, 'taking owls to Athens,' similar to the English 'taking coals to Newcastle.'

PISTHETAERUS

Here is the magpie, the turtle-dove, the swallow, the horned owl, the buzzard, the pigeon, the falcon, the ring-dove, the cuckoo, the red-foot, the red-cap, the purple-cap, the kestrel, the diver, the ousel, the osprey, the woodpecker.

EUELPIDES

Oh! oh! what a lot of birds! what a quantity of blackbirds! how they scold, how they come rushing up! What a noise! what a noise! Can they be bearing us ill-will? Oh! there! there! they are opening their beaks and staring at us.

PISTHETAERUS

Why, so they are.

CHORUS

Popopopopopopopopoi. Where is he who called me? Where am I to find him?

EPOPS

I have been waiting for you this long while! I never fail in my word to my friends.

CHORUS

Titititititititi. What good thing have you to tell me?

EPOPS

Something that concerns our common safety, and that is just as pleasant as it is to the purpose. Two men, who are subtle reasoners, have come here to seek me.

CHORUS

Where? What? What are you saying?

EPOPS

I say, two old men have come from the abode of men to propose a vast and splendid scheme to us.

CHORUS

Oh! 'tis a horrible, unheard-of crime! What are you saying?

EPOPS

Nay! never let my words scare you.

CHORUS
What have you done then?

EPOPS
I have welcomed two men, who wish to live with us.

CHORUS
And you have dared to do that!

EPOPS
Aye, and am delighted at having done so.

CHORUS
Where are they?

EPOPS
In your midst, as I am.

CHORUS
Ah! ah! we are betrayed; 'tis sacrilege! Our friend, he who picked up corn-seeds in the same plains as ourselves, has violated our ancient laws; he has broken the oaths that bind all birds; he has laid a snare for me, he has handed us over to the attacks of that impious race which, throughout all time, has never ceased to war against us. As for this traitorous bird, we will decide his case later, but the two old men shall be punished forthwith; we are going to tear them to pieces.

PISTHETAERUS
'Tis all over with us.

EUELPIDES
You are the sole cause of all our trouble. Why did you bring me from down yonder?

PISTHETAERUS
To have you with me.

EUELPIDES
Say rather to have me melt into tears.

PISTHETAERUS
Go to! you are talking nonsense.

EUELPIDES
How so?

PISTHETAERUS
How will you be able to cry when once your eyes are pecked out?

CHORUS
Io! io! forward to the attack, throw yourselves upon the foe, spill his blood; take to your wings and surround them on all sides. Woe to them! let us get to work with our beaks, let us devour them.

Nothing can save them from our wrath, neither the mountain forests, nor the clouds that float in the sky, nor the foaming deep. Come, peck, tear to ribbons. Where is the chief of the cohort? Let him engage the right wing.

EUELPIDES
This is the fatal moment. Where shall I fly to, unfortunate wretch that I am?

PISTHETAERUS
Stay! stop here!

EUELPIDES
That they may tear me to pieces?

PISTHETAERUS
And how do you think to escape them?

EUELPIDES
I don't know at all.

PISTHETAERUS
Come, I will tell you. We must stop and fight them. Let us arm ourselves with these stew-pots.

EUELPIDES
Why with the stew-pots?

PISTHETAERUS
The owl will not attack us.(1)

(1) An allusion to the Feast of Pots; it was kept at Athens on the third day of the Anthesteria, when all sorts of vegetables were stewed together and offered for the dead to Bacchus and Athene. This Feast was peculiar to Athens.—Hence Pisthetaerus thinks that the owl will recognize they are Athenians by seeing the stew-pots, and as he is an Athenian bird, he will not attack them.

EUELPIDES
But do you see all those hooked claws?

PISTHETAERUS
Seize the spit and pierce the foe on your side.

EUELPIDES
And how about my eyes?

PISTHETAERUS
Protect them with this dish or this vinegar-pot.

EUELPIDES
Oh! what cleverness! what inventive genius! You are a great general, even greater than Nicias, where stratagem is concerned.

CHORUS

Forward, forward, charge with your beaks! Come, no delay. Tear, pluck, strike, flay them, and first of all smash the stew-pot.

EPOPS
Oh, most cruel of all animals, why tear these two men to pieces, why kill them? What have they done to you? They belong to the same tribe, to the same family as my wife.(1)

(1) Procne, the daughter of Pandion, King of Athens.

CHORUS
Are wolves to be spared? Are they not our most mortal foes? So let us punish them.

EPOPS
If they are your foes by nature, they are your friends in heart, and they come here to give you useful advice.

CHORUS
Advice or a useful word from their lips, from them, the enemies of my forebears!

EPOPS
The wise can often profit by the lessons of a foe, for caution is the mother of safety. 'Tis just such a thing as one will not learn from a friend and which an enemy compels you to know. To begin with, 'tis the foe and not the friend that taught cities to build high walls, to equip long vessels of war; and 'tis this knowledge that protects our children, our slaves and our wealth.

CHORUS
Well then, I agree, let us first hear them, for 'tis best; one can even learn something in an enemy's school.

PISTHETAERUS
Their wrath seems to cool. Draw back a little.

EPOPS
'Tis only justice, and you will thank me later.

CHORUS
Never have we opposed your advice up to now.

PISTHETAERUS
They are in a more peaceful mood; put down your stew-pot and your two dishes; spit in hand, doing duty for a spear, let us mount guard inside the camp close to the pot and watch in our arsenal closely; for we must not fly.

EUELPIDES
You are right. But where shall we be buried, if we die?

PISTHETAERUS
In the Ceramicus;(1) for, to get a public funeral, we shall tell the Strategi that we fell at Orneae,(2) fighting the country's foes.

(1) A space beyond the walls of Athens which contained the gardens of the Academy and the graves of citizens who had died for their country.

(2) A town in Western Argolis, where the Athenians had been recently defeated. The somewhat similar work in Greek signifies 'birds.'

CHORUS
Return to your ranks and lay down your courage beside your wrath as the Hoplites do. Then let us ask these men who they are, whence they come, and with what intent. Here, Epops, answer me.

EPOPS
Are you calling me? What do you want of me?

CHORUS
Who are they? From what country?

EPOPS
Strangers, who have come from Greece, the land of the wise.

CHORUS
And what fate has led them hither to the land of the birds?

EPOPS
Their love for you and their wish to share your kind of life; to dwell and remain with you always.

CHORUS
Indeed, and what are their plans?

EPOPS
They are wonderful, incredible, unheard of.

CHORUS
Why, do they think to see some advantage that determines them to settle here? Are they hoping with our help to triumph over their foes or to be useful to their friends?

EPOPS
They speak of benefits so great it is impossible either to describe or conceive them; all shall be yours, all that we see here, there, above and below us; this they vouch for.

CHORUS
Are they mad?

EPOPS
They are the sanest people in the world.

CHORUS
Clever men?

EPOPS
The slyest of foxes, cleverness its very self, men of the world, cunning, the cream of knowing folk.

CHORUS

Tell them to speak and speak quickly; why, as I listen to you, I am beside myself with delight.

EPOPS

Here, you there, take all these weapons and hang them up inside close to the fire, near the figure of the god who presides there and under his protection; as for you, address the birds, tell them why I have gathered them together.

PISTHETAERUS

Not I, by Apollo, unless they agree with me as the little ape of an armourer agreed with his wife, not to bite me, nor pull me by the parts, nor shove things up my...

CHORUS

You mean the...

[Puts finger to bottom.]

Oh! be quite at ease.

PISTHETAERUS

No, I mean my eyes.

CHORUS

Agreed.

PISTHETAERUS

Swear it.

CHORUS

I swear it and, if I keep my promise, let judges and spectators give me the victory unanimously.

PISTHETAERUS

It is a bargain.

CHORUS

And if I break my word, may I succeed by one vote only.

HERALD

Hearken, ye people! Hoplites, pick up your weapons and return to your firesides; do not fail to read the decrees of dismissal we have posted.

CHORUS

Man is a truly cunning creature, but nevertheless explain. Perhaps you are going to show me some good way to extend my power, some way that I have not had the wit to find out and which you have discovered. Speak! 'tis to your own interest as well as to mine, for if you secure me some advantage, I will surely share it with you. But what object can have induced you to come among us? Speak boldly, for I shall not break the truce,—until you have told us all.

PISTHETAERUS

I am bursting with desire to speak; I have already mixed the dough of my address and nothing prevents me from kneading it.... Slave! bring the chaplet and water, which you must pour over my hands. Be quick!

EUELPIDES
Is it a question of feasting? What does it all mean?

PISTHETAERUS
By Zeus, no! but I am hunting for fine, tasty words to break down the hardness of their hearts.—I grieve so much for you, who at one time were kings...

CHORUS
We kings! Over whom?

PISTHETAERUS
...of all that exists, firstly of me and of this man, even of Zeus himself. Your race is older than Saturn, the Titans and the Earth.

CHORUS
What, older than the Earth!

PISTHETAERUS
By Phoebus, yes.

CHORUS
By Zeus, but I never knew that before!

PISTHETAERUS
'Tis because you are ignorant and heedless, and have never read your Aesop. 'Tis he who tells us that the lark was born before all other creatures, indeed before the Earth; his father died of sickness, but the Earth did not exist then; he remained unburied for five days, when the bird in its dilemma decided, for want of a better place, to entomb its father in its own head.

EUELPIDES
So that the lark's father is buried at Cephalae.

EPOPS
Hence, if we existed before the Earth, before the gods, the kingship belongs to us by right of priority.

EUELPIDES
Undoubtedly, but sharpen your beak well; Zeus won't be in a hurry to hand over his sceptre to the woodpecker.

PISTHETAERUS
It was not the gods, but the birds, who were formerly the masters and kings over men; of this I have a thousand proofs. First of all, I will point you to the cock, who governed the Persians before all other monarchs, before Darius and Megabyzus. 'Tis in memory of his reign that he is called the Persian bird.

EUELPIDES

For this reason also, even to-day, he alone of all the birds wears his tiara straight on his head, like the Great King.(1)

(1) All Persians wore the tiara, but always on one side; the Great King alone wore it straight on his head.

PISTHETAERUS
He was so strong, so great, so feared, that even now, on account of his ancient power, everyone jumps out of bed as soon as ever he crows at daybreak. Blacksmiths, potters, tanners, shoemakers, bathmen, corn-dealers, lyre-makers and armourers, all put on their shoes and go to work before it is daylight.

EUELPIDES
I can tell you something about that. 'Twas the cock's fault that I lost a splendid tunic of Phrygian wool. I was at a feast in town, given to celebrate the birth of a child; I had drunk pretty freely and had just fallen asleep, when a cock, I suppose in a greater hurry than the rest, began to crow. I thought it was dawn and set out for Alimos. I had hardly got beyond the walls, when a footpad struck me in the back with his bludgeon; down I went and wanted to shout, but he had already made off with my mantle.

PISTHETAERUS
Formerly also the kite was ruler and king over the Greeks.

EPOPS
The Greeks?

PISTHETAERUS
And when he was king, 'twas he who first taught them to fall on their knees before the kites.(1)

(1) The appearance of the kite in Greece betokened the return of springtime; it was therefore worshipped as a symbol of that season.

EUELPIDES
By Zeus! 'tis what I did myself one day on seeing a kite; but at the moment I was on my knees, and leaning backwards(1) with mouth agape, I bolted an obolus and was forced to carry my bag home empty.

PISTHETAERUS
The cuckoo was king of Egypt and of the whole of Phoenicia. When he called out "cuckoo," all the Phoenicians hurried to the fields to reap their wheat and their barley.

EUELPIDES
Hence no doubt the proverb, "Cuckoo! cuckoo! go to the fields, ye circumcised."(1)

(1) This was an Egyptian proverb, meaning, 'When the cuckoo sings we go harvesting.' Both the Phoenicians and the Egyptians practised circumcision.

PISTHETAERUS
So powerful were the birds that the kings of Grecian cities, Agamemnon, Menelaus, for instance, carried a bird on the tip of their sceptres, who had his share of all presents.

EUELPIDES

That I didn't know and was much astonished when I saw Priam come upon the stage in the tragedies with a bird, which kept watching Lysicrates(1) to see if he got any present.

(1) A general accused of treachery. The bird watches Lysicrates, because, according to Pisthetaerus, he had a right to a share of the presents.

PISTHETAERUS

But the strongest proof of all is, that Zeus, who now reigns, is represented as standing with an eagle on his head as a symbol of his royalty;(1) his daughter has an owl, and Phoebus, as his servant, has a hawk.

(1) It is thus that Phidias represents his Olympian Zeus.

EUELPIDES

By Demeter, 'tis well spoken. But what are all these birds doing in heaven?

PISTHETAERUS

When anyone sacrifices and, according to the rite, offers the entrails to the gods, these birds take their share before Zeus. Formerly men always swore by the birds and never by the gods; even now Lampon swears by the goose, when he wants to lie....Thus 'tis clear that you were great and sacred, but now you are looked upon as slaves, as fools, as Helots; stones are thrown at you as at raving madmen, even in holy places. A crowd of bird-catchers sets snares, traps, limed-twigs and nets of all sorts for you; you are caught, you are sold in heaps and the buyers finger you over to be certain you are fat. Again, if they would but serve you up simply roasted; but they rasp cheese into a mixture of oil, vinegar and laserwort, to which another sweet and greasy sauce is added, and the whole is poured scalding hot over your back, for all the world as if you were diseased meat.

CHORUS

Man, your words have made my heart bleed; I have groaned over the treachery of our fathers, who knew not how to transmit to us the high rank they held from their forefathers. But 'tis a benevolent Genius, a happy Fate, that sends you to us; you shall be our deliverer and I place the destiny of my little ones and my own in your hands with every confidence. But hasten to tell me what must be done; we should not be worthy to live, if we did not seek to regain our royalty by every possible means.

PISTHETAERUS

First I advise that the birds gather together in one city and that they build a wall of great bricks, like that at Babylon, round the plains of the air and the whole region of space that divides earth from heaven.

EPOPS

Oh, Cebriones! oh, Porphyrion!(1) what a terribly strong place!

(1) As if he were saying, "Oh, gods!" Like Lampon, he swears by the birds, instead of swearing by the gods.—The names of these birds are those of two of the Titans.

PISTHETAERUS

Then, this being well done and completed, you demand back the empire from Zeus; if he will not agree, if he refuses and does not at once confess himself beaten, you declare a sacred war against him and forbid the gods henceforward to pass through your country with lust, as hitherto, for the purpose of fondling their Alcmenas, their Alopes, or their Semeles!(1) if they try to pass through, you infibulate them with rings so that they can work no longer. You send another messenger to mankind, who will proclaim to them that the birds are kings, that for the future they must first of all sacrifice to them, and only afterwards to the gods; that it is fitting to appoint to each deity the bird that has most in common with it. For instance, are they sacrificing to Aphrodite, let them at the same time offer barley to the coot; are they immolating a sheep to Posidon, let them consecrate wheat in honour of the duck;(2) is a steer being offered to Heracles, let honey-cakes be dedicated to the gull;(3) is a goat being slain for King Zeus, there is a King-Bird, the wren,(4) to whom the sacrifice of a male gnat is due before Zeus himself even.

(1) Alcmena, wife of Amphitryon, King of Thebes and mother of Heracles.—Semele, the daughter of Cadmus and Hermione and mother of Bacchus; both seduced by Zeus.—Alope, daughter of Cercyon, a robber, who reigned at Eleusis and was conquered by Perseus. Alope was honoured with Posidon's caresses; by him she had a son named Hippothous, at first brought up by shepherds but who afterwards was restored to the throne of his grandfather by Theseus.

(2) Because water is the duck's domain, as it is that of Posidon.

(3) Because the gull, like Heracles, is voracious.

(4) The Germans still call it 'Zaunkonig' and the French 'roitelet,' both names thus containing the idea of 'king.'

EUELPIDES
This notion of an immolated gnat delights me! And now let the great Zeus thunder!

EPOPS
But how will mankind recognize us as gods and not as jays? Us, who have wings and fly?

PISTHETAERUS
You talk rubbish! Hermes is a god and has wings and flies, and so do many other gods. First of all, Victory flies with golden wings, Eros is undoubtedly winged too, and Iris is compared by Homer to a timorous dove. If men in their blindness do not recognize you as gods and continue to worship the dwellers in Olympus, then a cloud of sparrows greedy for corn must descend upon their fields and eat up all their seeds; we shall see then if Demeter will mete them out any wheat.

EUELPIDES
By Zeus, she'll take good care she does not, and you will see her inventing a thousand excuses.

PISTHETAERUS
The crows too will prove your divinity to them by pecking out the eyes of their flocks and of their draught-oxen; and then let Apollo cure them, since he is a physician and is paid for the purpose.

EUELPIDES
Oh! don't do that! Wait first until I have sold my two young bullocks.

PISTHETAERUS
If on the other hand they recognize that you are God, the principle of life, that you are Earth, Saturn, Posidon, they shall be loaded with benefits.

EPOPS

Name me one of these then.

PISTHETAERUS
Firstly, the locusts shall not eat up their vine-blossoms; a legion of owls and kestrels will devour them. Moreover, the gnats and the gall-bugs shall no longer ravage the figs; a flock of thrushes shall swallow the whole host down to the very last.

EPOPS
And how shall we give wealth to mankind? This is their strongest passion.

PISTHETAERUS
When they consult the omens, you will point them to the richest mines, you will reveal the paying ventures to the diviner, and not another shipwreck will happen or sailor perish.

EPOPS
No more shall perish? How is that?

PISTHETAERUS
When the auguries are examined before starting on a voyage, some bird will not fail to say, "Don't start! there will be a storm," or else, "Go! you will make a most profitable venture."

EUELPIDES
I shall buy a trading-vessel and go to sea, I will not stay with you.

PISTHETAERUS
You will discover treasures to them, which were buried in former times, for you know them. Do not all men say, "None knows where my treasure lies, unless perchance it be some bird."

EUELPIDES
I shall sell my boat and buy a spade to unearth the vessels.

EPOPS
And how are we to give them health, which belongs to the gods?

PISTHETAERUS
If they are happy, is not that the chief thing towards health? The miserable man is never well.

EPOPS
Old Age also dwells in Olympus. How will they get at it? Must they die in early youth?

PISTHETAERUS
Why, the birds, by Zeus, will add three hundred years to their life.

EPOPS
From whom will they take them?

PISTHETAERUS
From whom? Why, from themselves. Don't you know the cawing crow lives five times as long as a man?

EUELPIDES

Ah! ah! these are far better kings for us than Zeus!

PISTHETAERUS
Far better, are they not? And firstly, we shall not have to build them temples of hewn stone, closed with gates of gold; they will dwell amongst the bushes and in the thickets of green oak; the most venerated of birds will have no other temple than the foliage of the olive tree; we shall not go to Delphi or to Ammon to sacrifice; but standing erect in the midst of arbutus and wild olives and holding forth our hands filled with wheat and barley, we shall pray them to admit us to a share of the blessings they enjoy and shall at once obtain them for a few grains of wheat.

CHORUS
Old man, whom I detested, you are now to me the dearest of all; never shall I, if I can help it, fail to follow your advice. Inspirited by your words, I threaten my rivals the gods, and I swear that if you march in alliance with me against the gods and are faithful to our just, loyal and sacred bond, we shall soon have shattered their sceptre. 'Tis our part to undertake the toil, 'tis yours to advise.

EPOPS
By Zeus! 'tis no longer the time to delay and loiter like Nicias;(1) let us act as promptly as possible.... In the first place, come, enter my nest built of brushwood and blades of straw, and tell me your names.

(1) Nicias was commander, along with Demosthenes, and later on Alcibiades, of the Athenian forces before Syracuse, in the ill-fated Sicilian Expedition, 415-413 B.C. He was much blamed for dilatoriness and indecision.

PISTHETAERUS
That is soon done; my name is Pisthetaerus.

EPOPS
And his?

PISTHETAERUS
Euelpides, of the deme of Thria.

EPOPS
Good! and good luck to you.

PISTHETAERUS
We accept the omen.

EPOPS
Come in here.

PISTHETAERUS
Very well, 'tis you who lead us and must introduce us.

EPOPS
Come then.

PISTHETAERUS
Oh! my god! do come back here. Hi! tell us how we are to follow you. You can fly, but we cannot.

EPOPS

Well, well.

PISTHETAERUS

Remember Aesop's fables. It is told there, that the fox fared very ill, because he had made an alliance with the eagle.

EPOPS

Be at ease. You shall eat a certain root and wings will grow on your shoulders.

PISTHETAERUS

Then let us enter. Xanthias and Manes, pick up our baggage.

CHORUS

Hi! Epops! do you hear me?

EPOPS

What's the matter?

CHORUS

Take them off to dine well and call your mate, the melodious Procne, whose songs are worthy of the Muses; she will delight our leisure moments.

PISTHETAERUS

Oh! I conjure you, accede to their wish; for this delightful bird will leave her rushes at the sound of your voice; for the sake of the gods, let her come here, so that we may contemplate the nightingale.

EPOPS

Let it be as you desire. Come forth, Procne, show yourself to these strangers.

PISTHETAERUS

Oh! great Zeus! what a beautiful little bird! what a dainty form! what brilliant plumage!

EUELPIDES

Do you know how dearly I should like to splint her legs for her?

PISTHETAERUS

She is dazzling all over with gold, like a young girl.

EUELPIDES

Oh! how I should like to kiss her!

PISTHETAERUS

Why, wretched man, she has two little sharp points on her beak!

EUELPIDES

I would treat her like an egg, the shell of which we remove before eating it; I would take off her mask and then kiss her pretty face.

EPOPS

Let us go in.

PISTHETAERUS
Lead the way, and may success attend us.

CHORUS
Lovable golden bird, whom I cherish above all others, you, whom I associate with all my songs, nightingale, you have come, you have come, to show yourself to me and to charm me with your notes. Come, you, who play spring melodies upon the harmonious flute, lead off our anapaests.

Weak mortals, chained to the earth, creatures of clay as frail as the foliage of the woods, you unfortunate race, whose life is but darkness, as unreal as a shadow, the illusion of a dream, hearken to us, who are immortal beings, ethereal, ever young and occupied with eternal thoughts, for we shall teach you about all celestial matters; you shall know thoroughly what is the nature of the birds, what the origin of the gods, of the rivers, of Erebus, and Chaos; thanks to us, even Prodicus(1) will envy you your knowledge.

At the beginning there was only Chaos, Night, dark Erebus, and deep Tartarus. Earth, the air and heaven had no existence. Firstly, black-winged Night laid a germless egg in the bosom of the infinite deeps of Erebus, and from this, after the revolution of long ages, sprang the graceful Eros with his glittering golden wings, swift as the whirlwinds of the tempest. He mated in deep Tartarus with dark Chaos, winged like himself, and thus hatched forth our race, which was the first to see the light. That of the Immortals did not exist until Eros had brought together all the ingredients of the world, and from their marriage Heaven, Ocean, Earth and the imperishable race of blessed gods sprang into being. Thus our origin is very much older than that of the dwellers in Olympus. We are the offspring of Eros; there are a thousand proofs to show it. We have wings and we lend assistance to lovers. How many handsome youths, who had sworn to remain insensible, have not been vanquished by our power and have yielded themselves to their lovers when almost at the end of their youth, being led away by the gift of a quail, a waterfowl, a goose, or a cock.

And what important services do not the birds render to mortals! First of all, they mark the seasons for them, springtime, winter, and autumn. Does the screaming crane migrate to Libya,—it warns the husbandman to sow, the pilot to take his ease beside his tiller hung up in his dwelling,(2) and Orestes to weave a tunic, so that the rigorous cold may not drive him any more to strip other folk. When the kite reappears, he tells of the return of spring and of the period when the fleece of the sheep must be clipped. Is the swallow in sight? All hasten to sell their warm tunic and to buy some light clothing. We are your Ammon, Delphi, Dodona, your Phoebus Apollo. Before undertaking anything, whether a business transaction, a marriage, or the purchase of food, you consult the birds by reading the omens, and you give this name of omen(3) to all signs that tell of the future. With you a word is an omen, you call a sneeze an omen, a meeting an omen, an unknown sound an omen, a slave or an ass an omen.(4) Is it not clear that we are a prophetic Apollo to you? If you recognize us as gods, we shall be your divining Muses, through us you will know the winds and the seasons, summer, winter, and the temperate months. We shall not withdraw ourselves to the highest clouds like Zeus, but shall be among you and shall give to you and to your children and the children of your children, health and wealth, long life, peace, youth, laughter, songs and feasts; in short, you will all be so well off, that you will be weary and satiated with enjoyment.

Oh, rustic Muse of such varied note, tio, tio, tio, tiotinx, I sing with you in the groves and on the mountain tops, tio, tio, tio, tio, tiotinx.(5) I poured forth sacred strains from my golden throat in honour of the god Pan,) tio, tio, tio, tiotinx, from the top of the thickly leaved ash, and my voice mingles with the mighty choirs who extol Cybele on the mountain tops, totototototototinx. 'Tis to our concerts that Phrynichus comes to pillage like a bee the ambrosia of his songs, the sweetness of which so charms the ear, tio, tio, tio, tio, tinx.

If there be one of you spectators who wishes to spend the rest of his life quietly among the birds, let him come to us. All that is disgraceful and forbidden by law on earth is on the contrary honourable among us, the birds. For instance, among you 'tis a crime to beat your father, but with us 'tis an estimable deed; it's considered fine to run straight at your father and hit him, saying, "Come, lift your spur if you want to fight."(6) The runaway slave, whom you brand, is only a spotted francolin with us.(7) Are you Phrygian like Spintharus? Among us you would be the Phrygian bird, the goldfinch, of the race of Philemon. Are you a slave and a Carian like Execestides? Among us you can create yourself fore-fathers;(8) you can always find relations. Does the son of Pisias want to betray the gates of the city to the foe? Let him become a partridge, the fitting offspring of his father; among us there is no shame in escaping as cleverly as a partridge.

So the swans on the banks of the Hebrus, tio, tio, tio, tio, tiotinx, mingle their voices to serenade Apollo, tio, tio, tio, tio. tiotinx, flapping their wings the while, tio, tio, tio, tio, tiotinx; their notes reach beyond the clouds of heaven; all the dwellers in the forest stand still with astonishment and delight; a calm rests upon the waters, and the Graces and the choirs in Olympus catch up the strain, tio, tio, tio, tio, tiotinx.

There is nothing more useful nor more pleasant than to have wings. To begin with, just let us suppose a spectator to be dying with hunger and to be weary of the choruses of the tragic poets; if he were winged, he would fly off, go home to dine and come back with his stomach filled. Some Patroclides in urgent need would not have to soil his cloak, but could fly off, satisfy his requirements, and, having recovered his breath, return. If one of you, it matters not who, had adulterous relations and saw the husband of his mistress in the seats of the senators, he might stretch his wings, fly thither, and, having appeased his craving, resume his place. Is it not the most priceless gift of all, to be winged? Look at Diitrephes!(9) His wings were only wicker-work ones, and yet he got himself chosen Phylarch and then Hipparch; from being nobody, he has risen to be famous; 'tis now the finest gilded cock of his tribe.(10)

(1) A sophist of the island of Ceos, a disciple of Protagoras, as celebrated for his knowledge as for his eloquence. The Athenians condemned him to death as a corrupter of youth in 396 B.C.

(2) i.e. that it gave notice of the approach of winter, during which season the Ancients did not venture to sea.

(3) The Greek word for 'omen' is the same as that for 'bird.'

(4) A satire on the passion of the Greeks for seeing an omen in everything.

(5) An imitation of the nightingale's song.

(6) An allusion to cock-fighting; the birds are armed with brazen spurs.

(7) An allusion to the spots on this bird, which resemble the scars left by a branding iron.

(8) The Greek word here is also the name of a little bird.

(9) A basket-maker who had become rich.—The Phylarchs were the headmen of the tribes. They presided at the private assemblies and were charged with the management of the treasury.—The

Hipparchs, as the name implies, were the leaders of the cavalry; there were only two of these in the Athenian army.

(10) He had become a senator.

PISTHETAERUS
Halloa! What's this? By Zeus! I never saw anything so funny in all my life.(1)

*(1) **PISTHETAERUS** and **EUELPIDES** now both return with wings.*

EUELPIDES
What makes you laugh?

PISTHETAERUS
'Tis your bits of wings. D'you know what you look like? Like a goose painted by some dauber-fellow.

EUELPIDES
And you look like a close-shaven blackbird.

PISTHETAERUS
'Tis ourselves asked for this transformation, and, as Aeschylus has it, "These are no borrowed feathers, but truly our own."

EPOPS
Come now, what must be done?

PISTHETAERUS
First give our city a great and famous name, then sacrifice to the gods.

EUELPIDES
I think so too.

EPOPS
Let's see. What shall our city be called?

PISTHETAERUS
Will you have a high-sounding Laconian name? Shall we call it Sparta?

EUELPIDES
What! call my town Sparta? Why, I would not use esparto for my bed, even though I had nothing but bands of rushes.

PISTHETAERUS
Well then, what name can you suggest?

EUELPIDES
Some name borrowed from the clouds, from these lofty regions in which we dwell—in short, some well-known name.

PISTHETAERUS
Do you like Nephelococcygia?(1)

(1) A fanciful name constructed from (the word for) a cloud, and (the word for) a cuckoo; thus a city of clouds and cuckoos.

EPOPS
Oh! capital! truly 'tis a brilliant thought!

EUELPIDES
Is it in Nephelococcygia that all the wealth of Theovenes and most of Aeschines' is?

PISTHETAERUS
No, 'tis rather the plain of Phlegra, where the gods withered the pride of the sons of the Earth with their shafts.

EUELPIDES
Oh! what a splendid city! But what god shall be its patron? for whom shall we weave the peplus?(1)

(1) A sacred cloth, with which the statue of Athene in the Acropolis was draped.

PISTHETAERUS
Why not choose Athene Polias?

EUELPIDES
Oh! what a well-ordered town 'twould be to have a female deity armed from head to foot, while Clisthenes was spinning!

PISTHETAERUS
Who then shall guard the Pelargicon?(1)

(1) This was the name of the wall surrounding the Acropolis.

EPOPS
One of us, a bird of Persian strain, who is everywhere proclaimed to be the bravest of all, a true chick of Ares.

EUELPIDES
Oh! noble chick! What a well-chosen god for a rocky home!

PISTHETAERUS
Come! into the air with you to help the workers who are building the wall; carry up rubble, strip yourself to mix the mortar, take up the hod, tumble down the ladder, an you like, post sentinels, keep the fire smouldering beneath the ashes, go round the walls, bell in hand, and go to sleep up there yourself; then dispatch two heralds, one to the gods above, the other to mankind on earth and come back here.

EUELPIDES
As for yourself, remain here, and may the plague take you for a troublesome fellow!

PISTHETAERUS

Go, friend, go where I send you, for without you my orders cannot be obeyed. For myself, I want to sacrifice to the new god, and I am going to summon the priest who must preside at the ceremony. Slaves! slaves! bring forward the basket and the lustral water.

CHORUS
I do as you do, and I wish as you wish, and I implore you to address powerful and solemn prayers to the gods, and in addition to immolate a sheep as a token of our gratitude. Let us sing the Pythian chant in honour of the god, and let Chaeris accompany our voices.

PISTHETAERUS [To the **FLUTE-PLAYER**]
Enough! but, by Heracles! what is this? Great gods! I have seen many prodigious things, but I never saw a muzzled raven.(1)

(1) In allusion to the leather strap which flute-players wore to constrict the cheeks and add to the power of the breath. The performer here no doubt wore a raven's mask.

EPOPS
Priest! 'tis high time! Sacrifice to the new gods.

PRIEST
I begin, but where is he with the basket? Pray to the Vesta of the birds, to the kite, who presides over the hearth, and to all the god and goddess-birds who dwell in Olympus.

CHORUS
Oh! Hawk, the sacred guardian of Sunium, oh, god of the storks!

PRIEST
Pray to the swan of Delos, to Latona the mother of the quails, and to Artemis, the goldfinch.

PISTHETAERUS
'Tis no longer Artemis Colaenis, but Artemis the goldfinch.

PRIEST
And to Bacchus, the finch and Cybele, the ostrich and mother of the gods and mankind.

CHORUS
Oh! sovereign ostrich, Cybele, The mother of Cleocritus,(1) grant health and safety to the Nephelococcygians as well as to the dwellers in Chios...

(1) This Cleocritus, says the scholiast, was long-necked and strutted like an ostrich.

PISTHETAERUS
The dwellers in Chios! Ah! I am delighted they should be thus mentioned on all occasions.(1)

(1) The Chians were the most faithful allies of Athens, and hence their name was always mentioned in prayers, decrees, etc.

CHORUS
...to the heroes, the birds, to the sons of heroes, to the porphyrion, the pelican, the spoon-bill, the redbreast, the grouse, the peacock, the horned-owl, the teal, the bittern, the heron, the stormy petrel, the fig-pecker, the titmouse...

PISTHETAERUS

Stop! stop! you drive me crazy with your endless list. Why, wretch, to what sacred feast are you inviting the vultures and the sea-eagles? Don't you see that a single kite could easily carry off the lot at once? Begone, you and your fillets and all; I shall know how to complete the sacrifice by myself.

PRIEST

It is imperative that I sing another sacred chant for the rite of the lustral water, and that I invoke the immortals, or at least one of them, provided always that you have some suitable food to offer him; from what I see here, in the shape of gifts, there is naught whatever but horn and hair.

PISTHETAERUS

Let us address our sacrifices and our prayers to the winged gods.

A POET

Oh, Muse! celebrate happy Nephelococcygia in your hymns.

PISTHETAERUS

What have we here? Where did you come from, tell me? Who are you?

POET

I am he whose language is sweeter than honey, the zealous slave of the Muses, as Homer has it.

PISTHETAERUS

You a slave! and yet you wear your hair long?

POET

No, but the fact is all we poets are the assiduous slaves of the Muses, according to Homer.

PISTHETAERUS

In truth your little cloak is quite holy too through zeal! But, poet, what ill wind drove you here?

POET

I have composed verses in honour of your Nephelococcygia, a host of splendid dithyrambs and parthenians worthy of Simonides himself.

PISTHETAERUS

And when did you compose them? How long since?

POET

Oh! 'tis long, aye, very long, that I have sung in honour of this city.

PISTHETAERUS

But I am only celebrating its foundation with this sacrifice;(1) I have only just named it, as is done with little babies.

(1) This ceremony took place on the tenth day after birth, and may be styled the pagan baptism.

POET

"Just as the chargers fly with the speed of the wind, so does the voice of the Muses take its flight. Oh! thou noble founder of the town of Aetna, thou, whose name recalls the holy sacrifices, make us such gift as thy generous heart shall suggest."

PISTHETAERUS
He will drive us silly if we do not get rid of him by some present. Here! you, who have a fur as well as your tunic, take it off and give it to this clever poet. Come, take this fur; you look to me to be shivering with cold.

POET
My Muse will gladly accept this gift; but engrave these verses of Pindar's on your mind.

PISTHETAERUS
Oh! what a pest! 'Tis impossible then to be rid of him!

POET
"Straton wanders among the Scythian nomads, but has no linen garment. He is sad at only wearing an animal's pelt and no tunic." Do you conceive my bent?

PISTHETAERUS
I understand that you want me to offer you a tunic. Hi! you [To **EUELPIDES**], take off yours; we must help the poet.... Come, you, take it and begone.

POET
I am going, and these are the verses that I address to this city: "Phoebus of the golden throne, celebrate this shivery, freezing city; I have travelled through fruitful and snow-covered plains. Tralala! Tralala!"

PISTHETAERUS
What are you chanting us about frosts? Thanks to the tunic, you no longer fear them. Ah! by Zeus! I could not have believed this cursed fellow could so soon have learnt the way to our city. Come, priest, take the lustral water and circle the altar.

PRIEST
Let all keep silence!

A PROPHET
Let not the goat be sacrificed.

PISTHETAERUS
Who are you?

PROPHET
Who am I? A prophet.

PISTHETAERUS
Get you gone.

PROPHET
Wretched man, insult not sacred things. For there is an oracle of Bacis, which exactly applies to Nephelococcygia.

PISTHETAERUS

Why did you not reveal it to me before I founded my city?

PROPHET

The divine spirit was against it.

PISTHETAERUS

Well, 'tis best to know the terms of the oracle.

PROPHET

"But when the wolves and the white crows shall dwell together between Corinth and Sicyon..."

PISTHETAERUS

But how do the Corinthians concern me?

PROPHET

'Tis the regions of the air that Bacis indicated in this manner. "They must first sacrifice a white-fleeced goat to Pandora, and give the prophet, who first reveals my words, a good cloak and new sandals."

PISTHETAERUS

Are the sandals there?

PROPHET

Read. "And besides this a goblet of wine and a good share of the entrails of the victim."

PISTHETAERUS

Of the entrails—is it so written?

PROPHET

Read. "If you do as I command, divine youth, you shall be an eagle among the clouds; if not, you shall be neither turtle-dove, nor eagle, nor woodpecker."

PISTHETAERUS

Is all that there?

PROPHET

Read.

PISTHETAERUS

This oracle in no sort of way resembles the one Apollo dictated to me: "If an impostor comes without invitation to annoy you during the sacrifice and to demand a share of the victim, apply a stout stick to his ribs."

PROPHET

You are drivelling.

PISTHETAERUS

"And don't spare him, were he an eagle from out of the clouds, were it Lampon himself or the great Diopithes."

PROPHET

Is all that there?

PISTHETAERUS

Here, read it yourself, and go and hang yourself.

PROPHET

Oh! unfortunate wretch that I am.

PISTHETAERUS

Away with you, and take your prophecies elsewhere.

METON

I have come to you.

PISTHETAERUS

Yet another pest! What have you come to do? What's your plan? What's the purpose of your journey? Why these splendid buskins?

METON

I want to survey the plains of the air for you and to parcel them into lots.

PISTHETAERUS

In the name of the gods, who are you?

METON

Who am I? Meton, known throughout Greece and at Colonus.

PISTHETAERUS

What are these things?

METON

Tools for measuring the air. In truth, the spaces in the air have precisely the form of a furnace. With this bent ruler I draw a line from top to bottom; from one of its points I describe a circle with the compass. Do you understand?

PISTHETAERUS

Not the very least.

METON

With the straight ruler I set to work to inscribe a square within this circle; in its centre will be the market-place, into which all the straight streets will lead, converging to this centre like a star, which, although only orbicular, sends forth its rays in a straight line from all sides.

PISTHETAERUS

Meton, you new Thales...

METON

What d'you want with me?

PISTHETAERUS
I want to give you a proof of my friendship. Use your legs.

METON
Why, what have I to fear?

PISTHETAERUS
'Tis the same here as in Sparta. Strangers are driven away, and blows rain down as thick as hail.

METON
Is there sedition in your city?

PISTHETAERUS
No, certainly not.

METON
What's wrong then?

PISTHETAERUS
We are agreed to sweep all quacks and impostors far from our borders.

METON
Then I'm off.

PISTHETAERUS
I fear 'tis too late. The thunder growls already.

[Beats him.]

METON
Oh, woe! oh, woe!

PISTHETAERUS
I warned you. Now, be off, and do your surveying somewhere else.

[**METON** takes to his heels.]

AN INSPECTOR
Where are the Proxeni?

PISTHETAERUS
Who is this Sardanapalus?

INSPECTOR
I have been appointed by lot to come to Nephelococcygia as inspector.

PISTHETAERUS
An inspector! and who sends you here, you rascal?

INSPECTOR
A decree of Teleas.

PISTHETAERUS

Will you just pocket your salary, do nothing, and be off?

INSPECTOR

I' faith! that I will; I am urgently needed to be at Athens to attend the assembly; for I am charged with the interests of Pharnaces.

PISTHETAERUS

Take it then, and be off. See, here is your salary.

[Beats him.]

INSPECTOR

What does this mean?

PISTHETAERUS

'Tis the assembly where you have to defend Pharnaces.

INSPECTOR

You shall testify that they dare to strike me, the inspector.

PISTHETAERUS

Are you not going to clear out with your urns? 'Tis not to be believed; they send us inspectors before we have so much as paid sacrifice to the gods.

A DEALER IN DECREES

"If the Nephelococcygian does wrong to the Athenian..."

PISTHETAERUS

Now whatever are these cursed parchments?

DEALER IN DECREES

I am a dealer in decrees, and I have come here to sell you the new laws.

PISTHETAERUS

Which?

DEALER IN DECREES

"The Nephelococcygians shall adopt the same weights, measures and decrees as the Olophyxians."

PISTHETAERUS

And you shall soon be imitating the Ototyxians.

[Beats him.]

DEALER IN DECREES

Hullo! what are you doing?

PISTHETAERUS

Now will you be off with your decrees? For I am going to let YOU see some severe ones.

INSPECTOR [Returning]
I summon Pisthetaerus for outrage for the month of
Munychion..

PISTHETAERUS
Ha! my friend! are you still there?

DEALER IN DECREES
"Should anyone drive away the magistrates and not receive them, according to the decree duly
posted..."

PISTHETAERUS
What! rascal! you are there too?

INSPECTOR
Woe to you! I'll have you condemned to a fine of ten thousand drachmae.

PISTHETAERUS
And I'll smash your urns.

INSPECTOR
Do you recall that evening when you stooled against the column where the decrees are posted?

PISTHETAERUS
Here! here! let him be seized.

[The **INSPECTOR** runs off.]

Well! don't you want to stop any longer?

PRIEST
Let us get indoors as quick as possible; we will sacrifice the goat inside.

CHORUS
Henceforth it is to me that mortals must address their sacrifices and their prayers. Nothing escapes
my sight nor my might. My glance embraces the universe, I preserve the fruit in the flower by
destroying the thousand kinds of voracious insects the soil produces, which attack the trees and feed
on the germ when it has scarcely formed in the calyx; I destroy those who ravage the balmy terrace
gardens like a deadly plague; all these gnawing crawling creatures perish beneath the lash of my
wing. I hear it proclaimed everywhere: "A talent for him who shall kill Diagoras of Melos, and a talent
for him who destroys one of the dead tyrants." We likewise wish to make our proclamation: "A
talent to him among you who shall kill Philocrates, the Struthian; four, if he brings him to us alive.
For this Philocrates skewers the finches together and sells them at the rate of an obolus for seven.
He tortures the thrushes by blowing them out, so that they may look bigger, sticks their own
feathers into the nostrils of blackbirds, and collects pigeons, which he shuts up and forces them,
fastened in a net, to decoy others." That is what we wish to proclaim. And if anyone is keeping birds
shut up in his yard, let him hasten to let them loose; those who disobey shall be seized by the birds
and we shall put them in chains, so that in their turn they may decoy other men.

Happy indeed is the race of winged birds who need no cloak in winter! Neither do I fear the relentless rays of the fiery dog-days; when the divine grasshopper, intoxicated with the sunlight, when noon is burning the ground, is breaking out into shrill melody; my home is beneath the foliage in the flowery meadows. I winter in deep caverns, where I frolic with the mountain nymphs, while in spring I despoil the gardens of the Graces and gather the white, virgin berry on the myrtle bushes.

I want now to speak to the judges about the prize they are going to award; if they are favourable to us, we will load them with benefits far greater than those Paris received. Firstly, the owls of Laurium, which every judge desires above all things, shall never be wanting to you; you shall see them homing with you, building their nests in your money-bags and laying coins. Besides, you shall be housed like the gods, for we shall erect gables over your dwellings; if you hold some public post and want to do a little pilfering, we will give you the sharp claws of a hawk. Are you dining in town, we will provide you with crops. But, if your award is against us, don't fail to have metal covers fashioned for yourselves, like those they place over statues;(1) else, look out! for the day you wear a white tunic all the birds will soil it with their droppings.

(1) The Ancients appear to have placed metal discs over statues standing in the open air, to save them from injury from the weather, etc.

PISTHETAERUS
Birds! the sacrifice is propitious. But I see no messenger coming from the wall to tell us what is happening. Ah! here comes one running himself out of breath as though he were running the Olympic stadium.

MESSENGER
Where, where is he? Where, where, where is he? Where, where, where is he? Where is Pisthetaerus, our leader?

PISTHETAERUS
Here am I.

MESSENGER
The wall is finished.

PISTHETAERUS
That's good news.

MESSENGER
'Tis a most beautiful, a most magnificent work of art. The wall is so broad that Proxenides, the Braggartian, and Theogenes could pass each other in their chariots, even if they were drawn by steeds as big as the Trojan horse.

PISTHETAERUS
'Tis wonderful!

MESSENGER
Its length is one hundred stadia; I measured it myself.

PISTHETAERUS
A decent length, by Posidon! And who built such a wall?

MESSENGER

Birds—birds only; they had neither Egyptian brickmaker, nor stone-mason, nor carpenter; the birds did it all themselves; I could hardly believe my eyes. Thirty thousand cranes came from Libya with a supply of stones,(1) intended for the foundations. The water-rails chiselled them with their beaks. Ten thousand storks were busy making bricks; plovers and other water fowl carried water into the air.

(1) So as not to be carried away by the wind when crossing the sea, cranes are popularly supposed to ballast themselves with stones, which they carry in their beaks.

PISTHETAERUS

And who carried the mortar?

MESSENGER

Herons, in hods.

PISTHETAERUS

But how could they put the mortar into hods?

MESSENGER

Oh! 'twas a truly clever invention; the geese used their feet like spades; they buried them in the pile of mortar and then emptied them into the hods.

PISTHETAERUS

Ah! to what use cannot feet be put?

MESSENGER

You should have seen how eagerly the ducks carried bricks. To complete the tale, the swallows came flying to the work, their beaks full of mortar and their trowel on their back, just the way little children are carried.

PISTHETAERUS

Who would want paid servants after this? But tell me, who did the woodwork?

MESSENGER

Birds again, and clever carpenters too, the pelicans, for they squared up the gates with their beaks in such a fashion that one would have thought they were using axes; the noise was just like a dockyard. Now the whole wall is tight everywhere, securely bolted and well guarded; it is patrolled, bell in hand; the sentinels stand everywhere and beacons burn on the towers. But I must run off to clean myself; the rest is your business.

CHORUS

Well! what do you say to it? Are you not astonished at the wall being completed so quickly?

PISTHETAERUS

By the gods, yes, and with good reason. 'Tis really not to be believed. But here comes another messenger from the wall to bring us some further news! What a fighting look he has!

SECOND MESSENGER

Oh! oh! oh! oh! oh! oh!

PISTHETAERUS

What's the matter?

SECOND MESSENGER

A horrible outrage has occurred; a god sent by Zeus has passed through our gates and has penetrated the realms of the air without the knowledge of the jays, who are on guard in the daytime.

PISTHETAERUS

'Tis an unworthy and criminal deed. What god was it?

SECOND MESSENGER

We don't know that. All we know is, that he has got wings.

PISTHETAERUS

Why were not guards sent against him at once?

SECOND MESSENGER

We have dispatched thirty thousand hawks of the legion of Mounted Archers. All the hook-clawed birds are moving against him, the kestrel, the buzzard, the vulture, the great-horned owl; they cleave the air, so that it resounds with the flapping of their wings; they are looking everywhere for the god, who cannot be far away; indeed, if I mistake not, he is coming from yonder side.

PISTHETAERUS

All arm themselves with slings and bows! This way, all our soldiers; shoot and strike! Some one give me a sling!

CHORUS

War, a terrible war is breaking out between us and the gods! Come, let each one guard Air, the son of Erebus,(1) in which the clouds float. Take care no immortal enters it without your knowledge. Scan all sides with your glance. Hark! methinks I can hear the rustle of the swift wings of a god from heaven.

(1) Chaos, Night, Tartarus, and Erebus alone existed in the beginning; Eros was born from Night and Erebus, and he wedded Chaos and begot Earth, Air, and Heaven; so runs the fable.

PISTHETAERUS

Hi! you woman! where are you flying to? Halt, don't stir! keep motionless! not a beat of your wing!—Who are you and from what country? You must say whence you come.

IRIS

I come from the abode of the Olympian gods.

PISTHETAERUS

What's your name, ship or cap?

IRIS

I am swift Iris.

PISTHETAERUS

Paralus or Salaminia?(1)

(1) The names of the two sacred galleys which carried Athenian officials on State business.

IRIS
What do you mean?

PISTHETAERUS
Let a buzzard rush at her and seize her.

IRIS
Seize me! But what do all these insults mean?

PISTHETAERUS
Woe to you!

IRIS
'Tis incomprehensible.

PISTHETAERUS
By which gate did you pass through the wall, wretched woman?

IRIS
By which gate? Why, great gods, I don't know.

PISTHETAERUS
You hear how she holds us in derision. Did you present yourself to the officers in command of the jays? You don't answer. Have you a permit, bearing the seal of the storks?

IRIS
Am I awake?

PISTHETAERUS
Did you get one?

IRIS
Are you mad?

PISTHETAERUS
No head-bird gave you a safe-conduct?

IRIS
A safe-conduct to me, you poor fool!

PISTHETAERUS
Ah! and so you slipped into this city on the sly and into these realms of air-land that don't belong to you.

IRIS
And what other roads can the gods travel?

PISTHETAERUS

By Zeus! I know nothing about that, not I. But they won't pass this way. And you still dare to complain! Why, if you were treated according to your deserts, no Iris would ever have more justly suffered death.

IRIS
I am immortal.

PISTHETAERUS
You would have died nevertheless.—Oh! 'twould be truly intolerable! What! should the universe obey us and the gods alone continue their insolence and not understand that they must submit to the law of the strongest in their due turn? But tell me, where are you flying to?

IRIS
I? The messenger of Zeus to mankind, I am going to tell them to sacrifice sheep and oxen on the altars and to fill their streets with the rich smoke of burning fat.

PISTHETAERUS
Of which gods are you speaking?

IRIS
Of which? Why, of ourselves, the gods of heaven.

PISTHETAERUS
You, gods?

IRIS
Are there others then?

PISTHETAERUS
Men now adore the birds as gods, and 'tis to them, by Zeus, that they must offer sacrifices, and not to Zeus at all!

IRIS
Oh! fool! fool! Rouse not the wrath of the gods, for 'tis terrible indeed. Armed with the brand of Zeus, Justice would annihilate your race; the lightning would strike you as it did Licymnius and consume both your body and the porticos of your palace.

PISTHETAERUS
Here! that's enough tall talk. Just you listen and keep quiet! Do you take me for a Lydian or a Phrygian and think to frighten me with your big words? Know, that if Zeus worries me again, I shall go at the head of my eagles, who are armed with lightning, and reduce his dwelling and that of Amphion to cinders. I shall send more than six hundred porphyrions clothed in leopards' skins up to heaven against him; and formerly a single Porphyrion gave him enough to do. As for you, his messenger, if you annoy me, I shall begin by stretching your legs asunder, and so conduct myself, Iris though you be, that despite my age, you will be astonished. I will show you something that will make you three times over.

IRIS
May you perish, you wretch, you and your infamous words!

PISTHETAERUS

Won't you be off quickly? Come, stretch your wings or look out for squalls!

IRIS
If my father does not punish you for your insults...

PISTHETAERUS
Ha!... but just you be off elsewhere to roast younger folk than us with your lightning.

CHORUS
We forbid the gods, the sons of Zeus, to pass through our city and the mortals to send them the smoke of their sacrifices by this road.

PISTHETAERUS
'Tis odd that the messenger we sent to the mortals has never returned.

HERALD
Oh! blessed Pisthetaerus, very wise, very illustrious, very gracious, thrice happy, very... Come, prompt me, somebody, do.

PISTHETAERUS
Get to your story!

HERALD
All peoples are filled with admiration for your wisdom, and they award you this golden crown.

PISTHETAERUS
I accept it. But tell me, why do the people admire me?

HERALD
Oh you, who have founded so illustrious a city in the air, you know not in what esteem men hold you and how many there are who burn with desire to dwell in it. Before your city was built, all men had a mania for Sparta; long hair and fasting were held in honour, men went dirty like Socrates and carried staves. Now all is changed. Firstly, as soon as 'tis dawn, they all spring out of bed together to go and seek their food, the same as you do; then they fly off towards the notices and finally devour the decrees. The bird-madness is so clear, that many actually bear the names of birds. There is a halting victualler, who styles himself the partridge; Menippus calls himself the swallow; Opuntius the one-eyed crow; Philocles the lark; Theogenes the fox-goose; Lycurgus the ibis; Chaerephon the bat; Syracosius the magpie; Midias the quail; indeed he looks like a quail that has been hit hard over the head. Out of love for the birds they repeat all the songs which concern the swallow, the teal, the goose or the pigeon; in each verse you see wings, or at all events a few feathers. This is what is happening down there. Finally, there are more than ten thousand folk who are coming here from earth to ask you for feathers and hooked claws; so, mind you supply yourself with wings for the immigrants.

PISTHETAERUS
Ah! by Zeus, 'tis not the time for idling. Go as quick as possible and fill every hamper, every basket you can find with wings. Manes will bring them to me outside the walls, where I will welcome those who present themselves.

CHORUS
This town will soon be inhabited by a crowd of men.

PISTHETAERUS

If fortune favours us.

CHORUS

Folk are more and more delighted with it.

PISTHETAERUS

Come, hurry up and bring them along.

CHORUS

Will not man find here everything that can please him—wisdom, love, the divine Graces, the sweet face of gentle peace?

PISTHETAERUS

Oh! you lazy servant! won't you hurry yourself?

CHORUS

Let a basket of wings be brought speedily. Come, beat him as I do, and put some life into him; he is as lazy as an ass.

PISTHETAERUS

Aye, Manes is a great craven.

CHORUS

Begin by putting this heap of wings in order; divide them in three parts according to the birds from whom they came; the singing, the prophetic and the aquatic birds; then you must take care to distribute them to the men according to their character.

PISTHETAERUS [To **MANES**]

Oh! by the kestrels! I can keep my hands off you no longer; you are too slow and lazy altogether.

A PARRICIDE

Oh! might I but become an eagle, who soars in the skies! Oh! might I fly above the azure waves of the barren sea!

PISTHETAERUS

Ha! 'twould seem the news was true; I hear someone coming who talks of wings.

PARRICIDE

Nothing is more charming than to fly; I burn with desire to live under the same laws as the birds; I am bird-mad and fly towards you, for I want to live with you and to obey your laws.

PISTHETAERUS

Which laws? The birds have many laws.

PARRICIDE

All of them; but the one that pleases me most is, that among the birds it is considered a fine thing to peck and strangle one's father.

PISTHETAERUS

Aye, by Zeus! according to us, he who dares to strike his father, while still a chick, is a brave fellow.

PARRICIDE
And therefore I want to dwell here, for I want to strangle my father and inherit his wealth.

PISTHETAERUS
But we have also an ancient law written in the code of the storks, which runs thus, "When the stork father has reared his young and has taught them to fly, the young must in their turn support the father."

PARRICIDE
'Tis hardly worth while coming all this distance to be compelled to keep my father!

PISTHETAERUS
No, no, young friend, since you have come to us with such willingness, I am going to give you these black wings, as though you were an orphan bird; furthermore, some good advice, that I received myself in infancy. Don't strike your father, but take these wings in one hand and these spurs in the other; imagine you have a cock's crest on your head and go and mount guard and fight; live on your pay and respect your father's life. You're a gallant fellow! Very well, then! Fly to Thrace and fight.(1)

(1) The Athenians were then besieging Amphipolis in the Thracian Chalcidice.

PARRICIDE
By Bacchus! 'Tis well spoken; I will follow your counsel.

PISTHETAERUS
'Tis acting wisely, by Zeus.

CINESIAS
"On my light pinions I soar off to Olympus; in its capricious flight my Muse flutters along the thousand paths of poetry in turn..."

PISTHETAERUS
This is a fellow will need a whole shipload of wings.

CINESIAS [Singing]
"...and being fearless and vigorous, it is seeking fresh outlet."

PISTHETAERUS
Welcome, Cinesias, you lime-wood man! Why have you come here a-twisting your game leg in circles?

CINESIAS
"I want to become a bird, a tuneful nightingale."

PISTHETAERUS
Enough of that sort of ditty. Tell me what you want.

CINESIAS
Give me wings and I will fly into the topmost airs to gather fresh songs in the clouds, in the midst of the vapours and the fleecy snow.

PISTHETAERUS

Gather songs in the clouds?

CINESIAS

'Tis on them the whole of our latter-day art depends. The most brilliant dithyrambs are those that flap their wings in void space and are clothed in mist and dense obscurity. To appreciate this, just listen.

PISTHETAERUS

Oh! no, no, no!

CINESIAS

By Hermes! but indeed you shall. "I shall travel through thine ethereal empire like a winged bird, who cleaveth space with his long neck..."

PISTHETAERUS

Stop! easy all, I say!

CINESIAS

"...as I soar over the seas, carried by the breath of the winds..."

PISTHETAERUS

By Zeus! but I'll cut your breath short.

CINESIAS

"...now rushing along the tracks of Notus, now nearing Boreas across the infinite wastes of the ether."

[**PISTHETAERUS** beats him.]

Ah! old man, that's a pretty and clever idea truly!

PISTHETAERUS

What! are you not delighted to be cleaving the air?

CINESIAS

To treat a dithyrambic poet, for whom the tribes dispute with each other, in this style!

PISTHETAERUS

Will you stay with us and form a chorus of winged birds as slender as Leotrophides for the Cecropid tribe?

CINESIAS

You are making game of me, 'tis clear; but know that I shall never leave you in peace if I do not have wings wherewith to traverse the air.

AN INFORMER

What are these birds with downy feathers, who look so pitiable to me? Tell me, oh swallow with the long dappled wings.

PISTHETAERUS

Oh! but 'tis a regular invasion that threatens us. Here comes another of them, humming along.

INFORMER

Swallow with the long dappled wings, once more I summon you.

PISTHETAERUS

It's his cloak I believe he's addressing; 'faith, it stands in great need of the swallows' return.

INFORMER

Where is he who gives out wings to all comers?

PISTHETAERUS

'Tis I, but you must tell me for what purpose you want them.

INFORMER

Ask no questions. I want wings, and wings I must have.

PISTHETAERUS

Do you want to fly straight to Pellene?

INFORMER

I? Why, I am an accuser of the islands,(1) an informer...

(1) His trade was to accuse the rich citizens of the subject islands, and drag them before the Athenian court; he explains later the special advantages of this branch of the informer's business.

PISTHETAERUS

A fine trade, truly!

INFORMER

...a hatcher of lawsuits. Hence I have great need of wings to prowl round the cities and drag them before justice.

PISTHETAERUS

Would you do this better if you had wings?

INFORMER

No, but I should no longer fear the pirates; I should return with the cranes, loaded with a supply of lawsuits by way of ballast.

PISTHETAERUS

So it seems, despite all your youthful vigour, you make it your trade to denounce strangers?

INFORMER

Well, and why not? I don't know how to dig.

PISTHETAERUS

But, by Zeus! there are honest ways of gaining a living at your age without all this infamous trickery.

INFORMER

My friend, I am asking you for wings, not for words.

PISTHETAERUS
'Tis just my words that give you wings.

INFORMER
And how can you give a man wings with your words?

PISTHETAERUS
'Tis thus that all first start.

INFORMER
All?

PISTHETAERUS
Have you not often heard the father say to young men in the barbers' shops, "It's astonishing how Diitrephes' advice has made my son fly to horse-riding."—"Mine," says another, "has flown towards tragic poetry on the wings of his imagination."

INFORMER
So that words give wings?

PISTHETAERUS
Undoubtedly; words give wings to the mind and make a man soar to heaven. Thus I hope that my wise words will give you wings to fly to some less degrading trade.

INFORMER
But I do not want to.

PISTHETAERUS
What do you reckon on doing then?

INFORMER
I won't belie my breeding; from generation to generation we have lived by informing. Quick, therefore, give me quickly some light, swift hawk or kestrel wings, so that I may summon the islanders, sustain the accusation here, and haste back there again on flying pinions.

PISTHETAERUS
I see. In this way the stranger will be condemned even before he appears.

INFORMER
That's just it.

PISTHETAERUS
And while he is on his way here by sea, you will be flying to the islands to despoil him of his property.

INFORMER
You've hit it, precisely; I must whirl hither and thither like a perfect humming-top.

PISTHETAERUS
I catch the idea. Wait, i' faith, I've got some fine Corcyraean wings. How do you like them?

INFORMER

Oh! woe is me! Why, 'tis a whip!

PISTHETAERUS

No, no; these are the wings, I tell you, that set the top a-spinning.

INFORMER

Oh! oh! oh!

PISTHETAERUS

Take your flight, clear off, you miserable cur, or you will soon see what comes of quibbling and lying. Come, let us gather up our wings and withdraw.

CHORUS

In my ethereal flights I have seen many things new and strange and wondrous beyond belief. There is a tree called Cleonymus belonging to an unknown species; it has no heart, is good for nothing and is as tall as it is cowardly. In springtime it shoots forth calumnies instead of buds and in autumn it strews the ground with bucklers in place of leaves.

Far away in the regions of darkness, where no ray of light ever enters, there is a country, where men sit at the table of the heroes and dwell with them always—save always in the evening. Should any mortal meet the hero Orestes at night, he would soon be stripped and covered with blows from head to foot.

PROMETHEUS

Ah! by the gods! if only Zeus does not espy me! Where is Pisthetaerus?

PISTHETAERUS

Ha! what is this? A masked man!

PROMETHEUS

Can you see any god behind me?

PISTHETAERUS

No, none. But who are you, pray?

PROMETHEUS

What's the time, please?

PISTHETAERUS

The time? Why, it's past noon. Who are you?

PROMETHEUS

Is it the fall of day? Is it no later than that?

PISTHETAERUS

Oh! 'pon my word! but you grow tiresome.

PROMETHEUS

What is Zeus doing? Is he dispersing the clouds or gathering them?

PISTHETAERUS
Take care, lest I lose all patience.

PROMETHEUS
Come, I will raise my mask.

PISTHETAERUS
Ah! my dear Prometheus!

PROMETHEUS
Stop! stop! speak lower!

PISTHETAERUS
Why, what's the matter, Prometheus?

PROMETHEUS
H'sh! h'sh! Don't call me by my name; you will be my ruin, if Zeus should see me here. But, if you want me to tell you how things are going in heaven, take this umbrella and shield me, so that the gods don't see me.

PISTHETAERUS
I can recognize Prometheus in this cunning trick. Come, quick then, and fear nothing; speak on.

PROMETHEUS
Then listen.

PISTHETAERUS
I am listening, proceed!

PROMETHEUS
It's all over with Zeus.

PISTHETAERUS
Ah! and since when, pray?

PROMETHEUS
Since you founded this city in the air. There is not a man who now sacrifices to the gods; the smoke of the victims no longer reaches us. Not the smallest offering comes! We fast as though it were the festival of Demeter. The barbarian gods, who are dying of hunger, are bawling like Illyrians and threaten to make an armed descent upon Zeus, if he does not open markets where joints of the victims are sold.

PISTHETAERUS
What! there are other gods besides you, barbarian gods who dwell above Olympus?

PROMETHEUS
If there were no barbarian gods, who would be the patron of Execestides?

PISTHETAERUS
And what is the name of these gods?

PROMETHEUS

Their name? Why, the Triballi.

PISTHETAERUS

Ah, indeed! 'tis from that no doubt that we derive the word 'tribulation.'

PROMETHEUS

Most likely. But one thing I can tell you for certain, namely, that Zeus and the celestial Triballi are going to send deputies here to sue for peace. Now don't you treat, unless Zeus restores the sceptre to the birds and gives you Basileia in marriage.

PISTHETAERUS

Who is this Basileia?

PROMETHEUS

A very fine young damsel, who makes the lightning for Zeus; all things come from her, wisdom, good laws, virtue, the fleet, calumnies, the public paymaster and the triobolus.

PISTHETAERUS

Ah! then she is a sort of general manageress to the god.

PROMETHEUS

Yes, precisely. If he gives you her for your wife, yours will be the almighty power. That is what I have come to tell you; for you know my constant and habitual goodwill towards men.

PISTHETAERUS

Oh, yes! 'tis thanks to you that we roast our meat.

PROMETHEUS

I hate the gods, as you know.

PISTHETAERUS

Aye, by Zeus, you have always detested them.

PROMETHEUS

Towards them I am a veritable Timon; but I must return in all haste, so give me the umbrella; if Zeus should see me from up there, he would think I was escorting one of the Canephori.

PISTHETAERUS

Wait, take this stool as well.

CHORUS

Near by the land of the Sciapodes there is a marsh, from the borders whereof the odious Socrates evokes the souls of men. Pisander came one day to see his soul, which he had left there when still alive. He offered a little victim, a camel, slit his throat and, following the example of Ulysses, stepped one pace backwards.(4) Then that bat of a Chaerephon came up from hell to drink the camel's blood.

POSIDON

This is the city of Nephelococcygia, Cloud-cuckoo-town, whither we come as ambassadors. [To **TRIBALLUS**] Hi! what are you up to? you are throwing your cloak over the left shoulder. Come, fling it quick over the right! And why, pray, does it draggle in this fashion? Have you ulcers to hide like Laespodias? Oh! democracy! whither, oh! whither are you leading us? Is it possible that the gods have chosen such an envoy?

TRIBALLUS
Leave me alone.

POSIDON
Ugh! the cursed savage! you are by far the most barbarous of all the gods.—Tell me, Heracles, what are we going to do?

HERACLES
I have already told you that I want to strangle the fellow who has dared to block us in.

POSIDON
But, my friend, we are envoys of peace.

HERACLES
All the more reason why I wish to strangle him.

PISTHETAERUS
Hand me the cheese-grater; bring me the silphium for sauce; pass me the cheese and watch the coals.

HERACLES
Mortal! we who greet you are three gods.

PISTHETAERUS
Wait a bit till I have prepared my silphium pickle.

HERACLES
What are these meats?

PISTHETAERUS
These are birds that have been punished with death for attacking the people's friends.

HERACLES
And you are seasoning them before answering us?

PISTHETAERUS
Ah! Heracles! welcome, welcome! What's the matter?

HERACLES
The gods have sent us here as ambassadors to treat for peace.

A SERVANT
There's no more oil in the flask.

PISTHETAERUS
And yet the birds must be thoroughly basted with it.

HERACLES

We have no interest to serve in fighting you; as for you, be friends and we promise that you shall always have rain-water in your pools and the warmest of warm weather. So far as these points go we are armed with plenary authority.

PISTHETAERUS

We have never been the aggressors, and even now we are as well disposed for peace as yourselves, provided you agree to one equitable condition, namely, that Zeus yield his sceptre to the birds. If only this is agreed to, I invite the ambassadors to dinner.

HERACLES

That's good enough for me. I vote for peace.

POSIDON

You wretch! you are nothing but a fool and a glutton. Do you want to dethrone your own father?

PISTHETAERUS

What an error! Why, the gods will be much more powerful if the birds govern the earth. At present the mortals are hidden beneath the clouds, escape your observation, and commit perjury in your name; but if you had the birds for your allies, and a man, after having sworn by the crow and Zeus, should fail to keep his oath, the crow would dive down upon him unawares and pluck out his eye.

POSIDON

Well thought of, by Posidon!

HERACLES

My notion too.

PISTHETAERUS [To the **TRIBALLIAN**]

And you, what's your opinion?

TRIBALLUS

Nabaisatreu.

PISTHETAERUS

D'you see? he also approves. But hear another thing in which we can serve you. If a man vows to offer a sacrifice to some god, and then procrastinates, pretending that the gods can wait, and thus does not keep his word, we shall punish his stinginess.

POSIDON

Ah! ah! and how?

PISTHETAERUS

While he is counting his money or is in the bath, a kite will relieve him, before he knows it, either in coin or in clothes, of the value of a couple of sheep, and carry it to the god.

HERACLES

I vote for restoring them the sceptre.

POSIDON

Ask the Triballian.

HERACLES

Hi Triballian, do you want a thrashing?

TRIBALLUS

Saunaka baktarikrousa.

HERACLES

He says, "Right willingly."

POSIDON

If that be the opinion of both of you, why, I consent too.

HERACLES

Very well! we accord the sceptre.

PISTHETAERUS

Ah! I was nearly forgetting another condition. I will leave Here to Zeus, but only if the young Basileia is given me in marriage.

POSIDON

Then you don't want peace. Let us withdraw.

PISTHETAERUS

It matters mighty little to me. Cook, look to the gravy.

HERACLES

What an odd fellow this Posidon is! Where are you off to? Are we going to war about a woman?

POSIDON

What else is there to do?

HERACLES

What else? Why, conclude peace.

POSIDON

Oh! you ninny! do you always want to be fooled? Why, you are seeking your own downfall. If Zeus were to die, after having yielded them the sovereignty, you would be ruined, for you are the heir of all the wealth he will leave behind.

PISTHETAERUS

Oh! by the gods! how he is cajoling you. Step aside, that I may have a word with you. Your uncle is getting the better of you, my poor friend. The law will not allow you an obolus of the paternal property, for you are a bastard and not a legitimate child.

HERACLES

I a bastard! What's that you tell me?

PISTHETAERUS

Why, certainly; are you not born of a stranger woman? Besides, is not Athene recognized as Zeus' sole heiress? And no daughter would be that, if she had a legitimate brother.

HERACLES

But what if my father wished to give me his property on his death-bed, even though I be a bastard?

PISTHETAERUS

The law forbids it, and this same Posidon would be the first to lay claim to his wealth, in virtue of being his legitimate brother. Listen; thus runs Solon's law: "A bastard shall not inherit, if there are legitimate children; and if there are no legitimate children, the property shall pass to the nearest kin."

HERACLES

And I get nothing whatever of the paternal property?

PISTHETAERUS

Absolutely nothing. But tell me, has your father had you entered on the registers of his phratria?

HERACLES

No, and I have long been surprised at the omission.

PISTHETAERUS

What ails you, that you should shake your fist at heaven? Do you want to fight it? Why, be on my side, I will make you a king and will feed you on bird's milk and honey.

HERACLES

Your further condition seems fair to me. I cede you the young damsel.

POSIDON

But I, I vote against this opinion.

PISTHETAERUS

Then it all depends on the Triballian. [To the **TRIBALLIAN**] What do you say?

TRIBALLUS

Big bird give daughter pretty and queen.

HERACLES

You say that you give her?

POSIDON

Why no, he does not say anything of the sort, that he gives her; else I cannot understand any better than the swallows.

PISTHETAERUS

Exactly so. Does he not say she must be given to the swallows?

POSIDON

Very well! you two arrange the matter; make peace, since you wish it so; I'll hold my tongue.

HERACLES

We are of a mind to grant you all that you ask. But come up there with us to receive Basileia and the celestial bounty.

PISTHETAERUS

Here are birds already cut up, and very suitable for a nuptial feast.

HERACLES

You go and, if you like, I will stay here to roast them.

PISTHETAERUS

You to roast them! you are too much the glutton; come along with us.

HERACLES

Ah! how well I would have treated myself!

PISTHETAERUS

Let someone bring me a beautiful and magnificent tunic for the wedding.

CHORUS

At Phanae, near the Clepsydra, there dwells a people who have neither faith nor law, the Englottogastors, who reap, sow, pluck the vines and the figs with their tongues; they belong to a barbaric race, and among them the Philippi and the Gorgiases are to be found; 'tis these Englottogastorian Philippi who introduced the custom all over Attica of cutting out the tongue separately at sacrifices.

A MESSENGER

Oh, you, whose unbounded happiness I cannot express in words, thrice happy race of airy birds, receive your king in your fortunate dwellings. More brilliant than the brightest star that illumes the earth, he is approaching his glittering golden palace; the sun itself does not shine with more dazzling glory. He is entering with his bride at his side, whose beauty no human tongue can express; in his hand he brandishes the lightning, the winged shaft of Zeus; perfumes of unspeakable sweetness pervade the ethereal realms. 'Tis a glorious spectacle to see the clouds of incense wafting in light whirlwinds before the breath of the Zephyr! But here he is himself. Divine Muse! let thy sacred lips begin with songs of happy omen.

CHORUS

Fall back! to the right! to the left! advance! Fly around this happy mortal, whom Fortune loads with her blessings. Oh! oh! what grace! what beauty! Oh, marriage so auspicious for our city! All honour to this man! 'tis through him that the birds are called to such glorious destinies. Let your nuptial hymns, your nuptial songs, greet him and his Basileia! 'Twas in the midst of such festivities that the Fates formerly united Olympian Here to the King who governs the gods from the summit of his inaccessible throne. Oh! Hymen! oh! Hymenaeus! Rosy Eros with the golden wings held the reins and guided the chariot; 'twas he, who presided over the union of Zeus and the fortunate Here. Oh! Hymen! oh! Hymenaeus!

PISTHETAERUS

I am delighted with your songs, I applaud your verses. Now celebrate the thunder that shakes the earth, the flaming lightning of Zeus and the terrible flashing thunderbolt.

CHORUS

Oh, thou golden flash of the lightning! oh, ye divine shafts of flame, that Zeus has hitherto shot forth! Oh, ye rolling thunders, that bring down the rain! 'Tis by the order of OUR king that ye shall now stagger the earth! Oh, Hymen! 'tis through thee that he commands the universe and that he makes Basileia, whom he has robbed from Zeus, take her seat at his side. Oh! Hymen! oh! Hymenaeus!

PISTHETAERUS
Let all the winged tribes of our fellow-citizens follow the bridal couple to the palace of Zeus and to the nuptial couch! Stretch forth your hands, my dear wife! Take hold of me by my wings and let us dance; I am going to lift you up and carry you through the air.

CHORUS
Oh, joy! Io Paean! Tralala! victory is thing, oh, thou greatest of the gods!

Aristophanes – A Short Biography

Of Aristophanes, the greatest comedian of his age, and perhaps of all the ages, history contains few notices, and these of doubtful credit. Even the dates of his birth and death can only be inferred from his works, the former being estimated at 456 B.C. and the latter at 380. Many cities claimed the honor of giving him birth, the most probable story making him the son of Philippus of Ægina, and therefore only an adopted citizen of Athens. On this point some confusion has arisen from an attempt of Cleon to deprive Aristophanes of his civic rights, on the ground of illegitimacy, in revenge for his frequent invectives. The charge was disproved, thus pointing to the Athenian parentage of the comic poet, though as to this there is no trustworthy evidence. He was doubtless educated at Athens, and among other advantages is said to have been a disciple of Prodicus, though in his mention of that sophist he shows none of the respect due to his reputed master.

It was under the mighty genius of Aristophanes that the old Attic comedy received its fullest development. Dignified by the acquisition of a chorus of masked actors, and of scenery and machinery, and by a corresponding literary elaboration and elegance of style, comedy nevertheless remained true both to its origin and to the purposes of its introduction into the free imperial city. It borrowed much from tragedy, but it retained the Phallic abandonment of the old rural festivals, the license of word and gesture, and the audacious directness of personal invective. These characteristics are not features peculiar to Aristophanes. He was twitted by some of the older comic poets with having degenerated from the full freedom of the art through a tendency to refinement, and he took credit to himself for having superseded the time-honored can can and the stale practical joking of his predecessors by a nobler kind of mirth. But in boldness, as he likewise boasted, he had no peer; and the shafts of his wit, though dipped in wine-lees and at times feathered from very obscene fowl, flew at high game. He has been accused of seeking to degrade what he ought to have recognized as good; and it has been shown by competent critics that he is not to be taken as an impartial or accurate authority on Athenian history. But, partisan as he was, he was also a genuine patriot, and his very political sympathies—which were conservative—were such as have often stimulated the most effective political satire, because they imply an antipathy to every species of excess. Of reverence he was, however, altogether devoid; and his love for Athens was that of the most free-spoken of sons. Flexible, even in his religious notions, he was in this, as in other respects, ready to be educated by his times; and, like a true comic poet, he could be witty at the expense even of his friends, and, it might almost be said, of himself. In wealth of fancy and in beauty of lyric melody he ranks high among the great poets of all times.

It has been said that Aristophanes was an unmannerly buffoon, and so, indeed, he was, among his other faults. Nor was he at all justified in stooping to this degradation, whether it were that he was instigated by coarse inclinations, or that he held it necessary to gain over the populace, that he might have it in his power to tell such bold truths to the people. At least he makes it his boast that he did not court the laughter of the multitude so much as his rivals did, by mere indecent buffoonery, and that in this respect he brought his art to perfection. Not to be unreasonable, we should judge him from the standpoint of his own times, in respect of those peculiarities which make him offensive to us. On certain points, the ancients had quite a different morality from ours, and certainly a much freer one. This arose from their religion, which was a real worship of Nature, and had given sanctity to many public ceremonies which grossly violate decency. Moreover, as in consequence of the seclusion of their women, the men were almost always together, a certain coarseness entered into their conversation, as in such circumstances is apt to be the case.

The strongest testimony in favor of Aristophanes is that of Plato, who, in one of his epigrams, says that "the Graces chose his soul for their abode." The philosopher was a constant reader of the comedian, sending to Dionysius the elder a copy of the Clouds, from which to make himself acquainted with the Athenian republic. This was not intended merely as a description of the unbridled democratic freedom then prevailing at Athens, but as an example of the poet's thorough knowledge of the world, and of the political conditions of what was then the world's metropolis.

In his Symposium, Plato makes Aristophanes deliver a discourse on love, which the latter explains in a sensual manner, but with remarkable originality. At the end of the banquet, Aristodemus, who was one of the guests, fell asleep, "and, as the nights were long, took a good rest. When he was awakened, toward daybreak, by the crowing of cocks, the others were also asleep or had gone away, and there remained awake only Aristophanes, Agathon and Socrates, who were drinking out of a large goblet that was passed around, while Socrates was discoursing to them. Aristodemus did not hear all the discourse, for he was only half awake; but he remembered Socrates insisting to the other two that the genius of comedy was the same as that of tragedy, and that the writer of the one should also be a writer of the other. To this they were compelled to assent, being sleepy, and not quite understanding what he meant. And first Aristophanes fell asleep, and then, when the day was dawning, Agathon."

The words applied by Goethe to a shrewd adventurer, "mad, but clever," might also be used of the plays of Aristophanes, which are the very intoxication of poetry, the Bacchanalia of mirth. For mirth will maintain its rights as well as the other faculties; therefore, different nations have set apart certain holidays for jovial folly, and such as their saturnalia, their carnival, that being once satisfied to their hearts' content, they might keep themselves sober all the rest of the year, and leave free room for serious occupation. The old comedy is a general masquerade of the world, beneath which there passes much that is not allowed by the common rules of propriety; but at the same time much that is amusing, clever, and even instructive is brought to light, which would not have been possible but for the demolition for the moment of these barricades.

However corrupt and vulgar Aristophanes may have been in his personal propensities, however much he may offend decency and taste in his individual jests, yet in the plan and conduct of his poems in general, we cannot refuse him the praise of the carefulness and masterly skill of the finished artist. His language is infinitely graceful; the purest Atticism prevails in it, and he adapts it with great skill to all tones, from the most familiar dialogue to the lofty flight of the dithyrambic ode. We cannot doubt that he would have also succeeded in more serious poetry, when we see how at times he lavishes it, merely to annihilate its impression immediately afterward. This elegance is rendered the more attractive by contrast, since on the one hand he admist the rudest expressions of the people, the dialects, and even the mutilated Greek of barbarians, while on the other, the same arbitrary caprice which he brought to his views of universal nature and the human world, he also applies to language, and by composition, by allusion and personal names, or imitation of sound, forms the strangest words imaginable. His versification is not less artificial than that of the tragedians; he uses the same forms, but otherwise modified, as his personages are not to be impressive and dignified, but of a light and varied character; yet with all this seeming irregularity he observes the laws of metre no less strictly than the tragic poets do.

As we cannot help recognizing in Aristophanes' exercise of his varied and multiform art, the richest development of almost every poetical talent, so the extraordinary capacities of his hearers, which may be inferred from the structure of his works, are at every fresh perusal a matter of astonishment. Accurate acquaintance with the history and constitution of their country, with public events and proceedings, with the personal circumstances of almost all remarkable contemporaries, might be expected from the citizens of a democratic republic. But, besides this, Aristophanes required from his audience much poetic culture; especially they had to retain in their memories the tragic masterpieces, almost word by word, in order to understand his parodies.

The old comedy of the Greeks would have been impossible under any other form of government than a complete and unrestricted democracy; for it exercised a satirical censorship unsparing of public and private life, of statesmanship, of political and social usage, of education and literature, in a word, of everything which concerned the city, or could amuse the citizens. Retaining all the license, the riot and exuberance which marked its origin, it combined with this an expression of public opinion in such form that neither vice, misconduct, nor folly could venture to disregard it. If it was disfigured by grossness and licentiousness, this, it must be remembered, was in keeping with the sentiment of Dionysian festivals, just as a decorous cheerfulness was expected at festivals in honor of Apollo or Athena. To omit these features from comedy would be to deprive it of its most popular element, and without them the entertainment would have fallen flat.

Greek literature was immeasurably rich in this department: the names of the lost comedians, most of whom were very prolific, and of their works, so far as we are acquainted with them, would alone form a bulky catalogue. Although the new comedy unfolded itself, and flourished only for some eighty years, the number of plays certainly amounted to a thousand at least; but time has made such havoc with this superabundance of works that nothing remains except detached fragments in the original language, in many cases so disfigured as to be unintelligible, and in the Latin, a number of translations or adaptations of Greek originals.

For a comic poet who was unquestionably at the head of the fraternity, and in sentiment was intensely patriotic, the consciousness of his recognized power and the desire to use it for the good of his native city must ever have been the prevailing motives. At Athens such a man held an influence resembling rather that of the modern journalist than the modern dramatist; but the established type of comedy gave him an instrument such as no public satirist ever wielded, before or since. He was under no such limitations as to form or process, allusion or emphasis, as is the modern dramatist, and could indulge in the wildest flights of extravagance. After his keenest thrust or most passionate appeal, he could at once change his subject from the grave to the burlesque, and, in short, there was no limit to his field for invective and satire.

"Aristophanes," as one of his critics remarks, "is for us, the representative of old comedy." But it is important to notice that his genius, while it includes, also transcends the genius of the old comedy. He can denounce the frauds of Cleon, he can vindicate the duty of Athens to herself and to her allies with a stinging scorn and a force of patriotic indignation which make the poet almost forgotten in the citizen. He can banter Euripides with an ingenuity of light mockery which makes it seem for the time as if the leading Aristophonic trait was the art of seeing all things from their prosaic side. Yet it is neither in the denunciation nor in the mockery that he is most individual. His truest and highest faculty is revealed by those wonderful bits of lyric writing in which he soars above everything that can move laughter or tears, and makes the clear air thrill with the notes of a song as free, as musical and as wild as that of the nightingale invoked by his own chorus in the Birds. The speech of True Logic in the Clouds, the praises of country life in the Peace, the serenade in the Eccleziazusae, the songs of the Spartan and Athenian maidens in the Lysistrata, above all, perhaps the chorus in the Frogs, the beautiful chant of the Initiated—these passages, and such as these, are the true glories of Aristophanes. They are the strains, not of an artist, but of one who warbles for pure gladness of heart in some place made bright by the presence of a god. Nothing else in Greek poetry has quite this wild sweetness of the woods. Of modern poets Shakespeare alone, perhaps, has it in combination with a like richness and fertility of fancy.

A sympathetic reader of Aristophanes can hardly fail to percieve that, while his political and intellectual tendencies are well marked, his opinions, in so far as they color his comedies, are too definite to reward, or indeed to tolerate, analysis. Aristophanes was a natural conservative. His ideal was the Athens of the Persian wars. He disapproved the policy which had made Athenian empire irksome to the allies and formidable to Greece; he detested the vulgarity and the violence of mob-rule; he clave to the old worship of the gods; he regarded the new ideas of education as a tissue of imposture and impiety. How far he was from clearness or precision of view in regard to the intellectual revolution which was going forward appears from the Clouds, in which thinkers and literary workers who had absolutely nothing in common are treated with sweeping ridicule as prophets of a common heresy. Aristophanes is one of the men for whom opinion is mainly a matter of feeling, not of reason. His imaginative susceptibility gave him a warm and loyal love for the traditional glories of Athens, however dim the past to which they belonged; a horror of what was offensive or absurd in pretension. The broad preferences and dislikes thus generated were enough not only to point the moral of comedy, but to make him, in many cases, a really useful censor for the city. The service which he could render in this way was, however, only negative. He could hardly be, in any positive sense, a political or a moral teacher for Athens. His rooted antipathy to intellectual progress, while it affords easy and wide scope for his wit, must, after all, lower his rank. The great minds are not the enemies of ideas. But as a mocker—to use the word which seems most closely to describe him on this side—he is incomparable for the union of subtlety with the riot of comic imagination. As a poet, he is immortal; and, amont Athenian poets, he has for his distinctive characteristic that he is inspired less by that Greek genius which never allows fancy to escape from the control of defining, though spiritualizing reason, than by such ethereal rapture of the unfettered fancy as lifts Shakespeare or Shelley above it,—

"Pouring out his full soul
In profuse strains of unpremeditated art."

Aristophanes – A Concise Bibliography

Surviving Plays

The Acharnians (425 BC)
The Knights (424 BC)
The Clouds (original 423 BC, uncompleted revised version from 419 BC – 416 BC survives)
The Wasps (422 BC)
Peace (first version, 421 BC)
The Birds (414 BC)
Lysistrata (411 BC)
Thesmophoriazusae or The Women Celebrating the Thesmophoria (first version c.411 BC)
The Frogs (405 BC)

Ecclesiazusae or The Assemblywomen; (c. 392 BC)
Wealth (second version, 388 BC)

Dated But Lost Plays

Banqueters (427 BC)
Babylonians (426 BC)
Farmers (424 BC)
Merchant Ships (423 BC)
Clouds (first version) (423 BC)
Proagon (422 BC)
Amphiaraus (A414 BC)
Plutus (first version, 408 BC)
Gerytades (probably 407 BC)
Cocalus (387 BC)
Aiolosicon (second version, 386 BC)

Undated Lost Plays
Aiolosicon (first version)
Anagyrus
Frying-Pan Men
Daedalus
Danaids
Centaur
Heroes
Lemnian Women
Old Age
Peace (second version)
Phoenician Women
Polyidus
Seasons
Storks
Telemessians
Triphales
Thesmophoriazusae (Women at the Thesmophoria Festival, second version)
Women in Tents

www.ingramcontent.com/pod-product-compliance
Lightning Source LLC
Chambersburg PA
CBHW060051050426
42448CB00011B/2393